First Look at...
DOS 6.0
Ruth Schmitz

McGraw-Hill, Inc.
New York   St. Louis   San Francisco   Auckland   Bogotá
Caracas   Lisbon   London   Madrid   Mexico City   Milan
Montreal   New Delhi   San Juan   Singapore
Sydney   Tokyo   Toronto

Mitchell **McGRAW-HILL**
Watsonville, CA 95076

First Look at DOS 6.0

Copyright © 1994 by **McGraw-Hill, Inc.** All rights reserved. Printed in the United States of America. Except as permitted under the United States Copyright Act of 1976, no part of this publication may be reproduced or distributed in any form or by any means, or stored in a database or retrieval system, without the prior written permission of the publisher.

567890 DOC/DOC 998765

ISBN 0-07-056880-4

Sponsoring editor: Roger Howell
Editorial assistant: Laurie Boudreau
Director of production: Jane Somers
Production supervisor: Leslie Austin
Project manager: Christi Payne Fryday, Bookman Productions
Interior designer: Renee Deprey
Cover designer: Janet Bollow
Cover photo: W. Warren/**West**light
Compositor: Bookman Productions
Printer and binder: R. R. Donnelley & Sons

Library of Congress Card Catalog No. 93-78718

Information has been obtained by Mitchell McGraw-Hill from sources believed to be reliable. However, because of the possibility of human or mechanical error by our sources, Mitchell McGraw-Hill, or others, Mitchell McGraw-Hill does not guarantee the accuracy, adequacy, or completeness of any information and is not responsible for any errors or omissions or the results obtained from use of such information.

This book is printed on acid-free paper.

Contents

Preface   vii

LESSON 1   Computer Components and DOS   1
Objectives   1
Computer Components   1
Cold Boot the Computer   3
Explore the Keyboard   5
Warm Boot the Computer   6
DATE and TIME   7
Special Keys   8
Summary of Commands   10
Review Questions   11
Hands-On Exercises   11

LESSON 2   DOS 6.0 Command Aids   12
Objectives   12
DOS Commands   12
PROMPT   14
PATH   14
FASTHELP   15
DOSKEY   16
Summary of Commands   19
Review Questions   19
Hands-On Exercises   20

LESSON 3   Disks and Drives   21
Objectives   21
Disk Drives   21
FORMAT   23
Change the Current Drive   27
Format Double-Density Disks in High-Density Drives   27
DIR (Directory)   27
  DIR Switches • List Files on a Target Drive
Summary of Commands   30
Review Questions   31
Hands-On Exercises   31

LESSON 4 Multidirectory Disks   33

Objectives   33
Filenames and Extensions   33
Wild-Card Characters   34
Multiple Directories   35
TREE   36
   Directory Names
CD (Current Directory/Change Directory)   37
   Current Directory • Change Directory
MD (Make a Directory)   38
RD (Remove a Directory)   41
DELTREE   42
Summary of Commands   43
Review Questions   44
Hands-On Exercises   44

LESSON 5 File Management   46

Objectives   46
COPY   46
MOVE   49
REN (Rename)   50
EDIT   51
TYPE   52
DEL (Delete)   52
UNDELETE   54
Summary of Commands   56
Review Questions   56
Hands-On Exercises   57

LESSON 6 Disk Management   59

Objectives   59
DISKCOPY   59
XCOPY   60
CHKDSK (Check Disk)   62
DEFRAG (Defragment)   63
SYS (System)   64
Summary of Commands   65
Review Questions   66
Hands-On Exercises   67

LESSON 7   DOS 6.0 Shell   68

Objectives   68
DOS Shell Basics   68
    Identifying Parts of the DOS Shell • Terminology
Explore the DOS Shell   71
Exit the DOS Shell   73
Menus, Dialog Boxes, and HELP   73
    Drop-Down Menus • Dimmed Commands • Dialog Boxes • HELP
DOS Shell Directory Tree   77
The File List Area   78
Summary of Commands   80
Review Questions   82
Hands-On Exercises   82

LESSON 8   DOS Shell Commands   84

Objectives   84
FORMAT   84
Directories   85
    Make a Directory • Rename a Directory • Remove a Directory
Copy and Move Files   88
    Copy • Move
Delete and Undelete Files   91
    Delete • Undelete • Change Disks
Run   92
Summary of Commands   93
Review Questions   94
Hands-On Exercises   94

LESSON 9   Edit   96

Objectives   96
Create a File   96
Modify a File   98
Summary of Commands   100
Review Questions   101
Hands-On Exercises   102

LESSON 10   Customize Your System   103

Objectives   103
MEM (Memory)   103
AUTOEXEC.BAT   104

@ECHO OFF 105
PATH 106
UNDELETE 108
Computer Viruses 108
CONFIG.SYS 109
  BREAK • FILES • BUFFERS • ANSI.SYS
Customized Booting 111
Summary of Commands 112
Review Questions 113
Hands-On Exercises 114

LESSON 11 — Macros and Batch Files — 115

Objectives 115
HELP 115
DOSKEY Macros 117
Batch Files 118
  REM (Remark) • PAUSE
Create a Batch File 119
ECHO 120
Summary of Commands 123
Review Questions 124
Hands-On Exercises 125

LESSON 12 — Advanced Commands — 126

Objectives 126
Associate Files 126
Program Groups and Items 129
MSD (Microsoft Diagnostics) 131
CONFIG.SYS Menu 132
Summary of Commands 134
Review Questions 134
Hands-On Exercises 135

Answers to Review Questions — 136
Answers to Hands-On Exercises — 138
DOS 6.0 Command Summary — 142
DOS Shell Commands — 145
Index — 147

Preface

First Look at DOS 6.0 is a self-paced, hands-on tutorial that covers the essential and most commonly used features of DOS 6.0. This book can be used:

- in a short course on DOS 6.0
- as a supplement in a microcomputer applications course
- as a supplement in a variety of business courses
- as a self-paced guide to DOS 6.0

Written in plain, simple English using step-by-step instructions, this book and other books in the First Look Series quickly get the reader "up to speed" with today's popular software packages in a minimum number of pages. Complete with a comprehensive Command Summary and a thorough Index, *First Look at DOS 6.0* makes reference quick and easy.

ORGANIZATION

First Look at DOS 6.0 begins with basic start-up information, then progresses to more advanced features of DOS 6.0. The following features aid learning in each lesson:

- **Objectives** provide an overview.
- **Step-by-step, hands-on tutorials** guide the reader through specific functions and commands.
- **Screen displays** monitor the reader's progress.
- **Summary of Commands** makes reference quick and easy.
- **Review Questions** reinforce key concepts.
- **Hands-On Exercises** require readers to apply the skills and concepts just learned.

As readers work through *First Look at DOS 6.0,* they create files that are used in later lessons. These files should be saved on a data disk so they can be easily located and retrieved. It is assumed that readers have access to the full-powered software package and all its features.

Use the First Look Series for brief and affordable coverage of today's most popular software applications packages.

ACKNOWLEDGMENTS

I appreciate and thank the following people for the excellent suggestions and comments in their reviews:

Glenna Stites, Johnson County Community College

Marcia Merrill, University of Nebraska at Kearney (UNK)

The thoroughness and depth of their reviews enabled me to make several improvements to this book.

The support and encouragement of colleagues at UNK, family, and friends greatly contributed to this book. Special thanks are also given to my friends Roger Howell, Laurie Boudreau, Leslie Austin, and Jane Somers at Mitchell McGraw-Hill and Christi Fryday at Bookman Productions—they were super to work with.

Ruth Schmitz
Kearney, Nebraska

# Computer Components and DOS

OBJECTIVES

In this lesson you will learn how to:

- Identify the parts of a computer system.
- Cold boot and warm boot a computer.
- Recognize the DOS or system prompt.
- Change the computer's date.
- Change the computer's time.
- Clear the computer screen.
- Identify how the computer keyboard differs from a typewriter keyboard.
- Cancel a command.
- Interrupt a command.
- Print the screen and have the printer mirror the screen.

What is **DOS**? DOS is a **disk operating system**. DOS 6.0 is a disk operating system used on IBM and IBM-compatible microcomputers. Every microcomputer (frequently called a PC for personal computer) must have an operating system. The operating system is made up of many small programs or files that are each designed to do a different task in controlling, coordinating, and managing all the components of a computer.

Two common operating systems are PC DOS and MS-DOS. PC DOS, written for IBM by Microsoft in prior versions, is usually run on IBM PCs. MS-DOS, also written by Microsoft, is usually installed on IBM-compatible PCs. With all the prior DOS versions, PC DOS and MS-DOS were quite similar. However, Microsoft is not writing PC DOS 6.0 for IBM. Though undoubtedly both PC DOS 6.0 and MS-DOS 6.0 will be similar, this text is written for MS-DOS 6.0.

COMPUTER COMPONENTS

Every microcomputer has four major hardware components: the central processing unit, keyboard, one or more disk drives, and a monitor. Figure 1-1 shows a typical microcomputer system. One of DOS's tasks is to coordinate all actions performed by the hardware.

Figure 1-1
A typical PC system

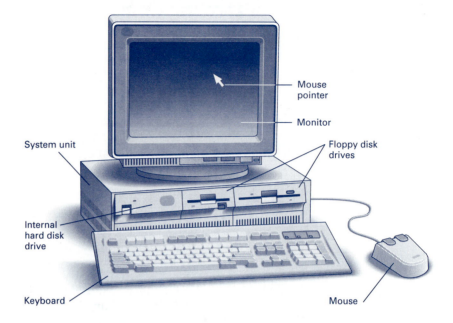

The **system unit** houses the **central processing unit (CPU)** and **memory**. Though some memory is reserved for special functions, most memory is available as a temporary working space (**RAM**, or **random access memory**) for programs, data, and commands. When the computer is turned off, the contents of RAM are erased.

Though the alphabetic portion of the PC **keyboard** is identical to that of the typewriter, the PC keyboard has several special keys. As you explore the keyboard, you'll become familiar with the special keys and how the PC keyboard differs from that of the typewriter.

Disk drives are the hardware components that read and write on magnetic disks. Disk drives on IBM and IBM-compatible microcomputers are referred to by letter (A, B, C, etc.). Drive A and drive B refer to the disk drives for floppy (removable) disks. Drive C refers to the drive for the hard (internal) disk. Each drive has a small light that goes on to show when the computer is reading or writing data to the disk in that drive.

A command entered via the keyboard appears on the **monitor** (screen). The output of some DOS commands also appears on the monitor. Together, the monitor and keyboard are called a **console**.

Though not an integral part of a computer, most users think of a **printer** as essential hardware. Printers are available from inexpensive dot-matrix printers to expensive laser printers.

A **mouse** is a hand-held device that helps you interact with a program. A mouse can only be used with programs specifically designed for it. The DOS 6.0 Shell, introduced in Lesson Seven, accepts commands by pointing and clicking with the mouse.

COLD BOOT THE COMPUTER

Cold boot describes turning the computer on, as it literally has to pull itself up from scratch. During a cold boot, the PC does a self-diagnostic test of memory, the microprocessor chip, the electronics, and reset devices. Next the computer looks for a disk containing the operating system booting files and loads them into memory. As all this happens, you may notice text or numbers on the screen as your system performs the diagnostic tests.

To cold boot your computer:

1. Locate the off/on switch or button on the CPU. Turn your computer on. Your floppy disk drive(s) should be empty.

2. Your monitor may also have an off/on switch or button. If so, turn your monitor on.

Watch the disk drive lights on your CPU. After the self-diagnostic tests, your computer will look for the booting files on drive A. Your computer might be configured to also look for these files on drive B. Not finding a disk in drive A and/or drive B, the light for your hard drive comes on and the booting files are located and copied into memory. The disk with the booting files is called a **system disk**. The hard drive on your computer is a system disk.

The appearance of your screen depends on how your computer is configured or set up.

3. If your computer prompts you for the current date, press [Enter] (the key with the hooked arrow directly above [Shift] on the right part of the alphabetic keyboard). Entering the current date is covered later in this lesson.

4. If your computer prompts you for the current time, press [Enter]. Entering the current time is also covered later in this lesson.

5. If your computer boots to display a menu, follow the instructions on the screen to exit to the DOS prompt. Skip to step 8.

6. If your computer displays a screen similar to Figure 1-2, this is a Windows screen. Hold down [Alt] while you type **f**; type **x** and press [Enter]. Skip to step 8.

7. If your computer displays a screen similar to Figure 1-3, this is the DOS Shell. Press [F3] (the keys labeled F1 through F10 or F12 are above the alphabetic part of your keyboard or at the far left of the alphabetic part of your keyboard) to exit to the DOS prompt.

8. Type **cd ** and then press [Enter] (the key with the hooked arrow directly above [Shift] on the right part of the alphabetic keyboard).

9. Type **cls** and press [Enter]

4 First Look at DOS 6.0

Figure 1-2
Windows screen

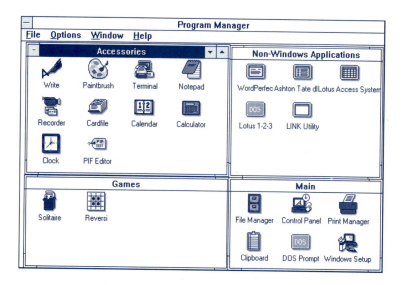

Figure 1-3
DOS Shell

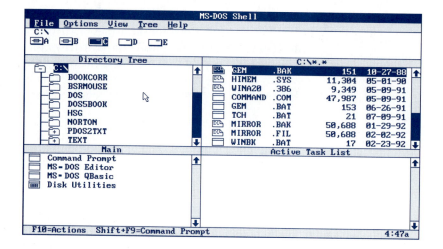

10. If C:\>_ is not displayed on your screen, type **prompt pg** and press Enter.

On the screen, the **C:** identifies your drive as drive C. (Drive letters are always followed by a colon.) Drive C is the **current drive**. This is the drive where DOS expects to find the files upon which it is to execute commands. The **backslash** (\) to the right of the C: identifies the current directory (division). The blinking underline (_) beside the C:\> is the **cursor**, which shows where the next typed character will appear. As you type a command, the cursor moves to the right. The > separates the cursor from the drive and directory information.

The C:\>_ is called a **system prompt** or **DOS prompt** because DOS, the operating system, is prompting you to enter a command. As you type a command at the DOS prompt, where you type is also referred to as the **command line**.

EXPLORE THE KEYBOARD

When entering a command, nothing happens until [Enter] is pressed. Pressing [Enter] tells DOS that the command being entered is complete. DOS is not case-sensitive. It accepts commands in either uppercase or lowercase letters.

To explore the keyboard:

1. Type **dir** and press [Enter]

   A list of files on the current drive (drive C) appears on the screen. You may have so many files that some names disappear off the top of your screen. This is called **scrolling**.

2. Press [Caps Lock] once so that the next command you enter will be in all capital letters.

3. Type **CLS** and press [Enter]. The CLS command clears the screen and moves the cursor to the upper-left corner.

4. Type **DIR** and press [Enter]. Look at your screen. The letters you typed should be in uppercase. As this is the same command you typed in step 1, you can see that DOS accepts commands in either uppercase or lowercase letters.

5. Type **DIR C*.*** and press [Enter] to list all files starting with the letter C. In order to type a symbol on the upper portion of a key, you must hold down [Shift].

6. Hold down [Shift] while you type **DIR** and press [Enter]. [Shift] counteracted [Caps Lock]. Dir appears in lowercase, not uppercase.

7. Type **ABC 123** and press [Enter]. After pressing [Enter], the screen displays the message "Bad command or file name". This is a common error message. DOS is telling you that it does not recognize the command you entered.

NOTE: *As you are exploring the keyboard rather than entering DOS commands, ignore the "Bad command or file name" error message.*

8. Clear your screen by typing **CLS** and pressing [Enter]

To explore the numeric keypad:

1. Type **147** on the numeric keypad. Most computers are set up so the numeric keypad is on (will let you type numbers) when the computer is booted. Press [Enter]

2. Press [Num Lock]

3. Again type **147** on the numeric keypad. Nothing happens. The numeric keypad is now set for moving the cursor with the arrow keys.

4. Enter the command to clear your screen.

The computer has several keys or key combinations that are called **toggle keys**. A toggle key turns something on or off. The button on a TV remote control is a toggle key. The same button is pushed to turn the TV on and to turn the TV off. A toggle key is used when there are only two possible conditions—on or off.

[Caps Lock] is a toggle key that changes letters to uppercase (caps on) or lowercase (caps off). [Num Lock] is also a toggle key. It is used to toggle the numeric keypad between entering numbers (numbers on) and moving the cursor (numbers off).

WARM BOOT THE COMPUTER

Restarting the computer when it is already on is called a **warm boot**. A warm boot does not erase or change disk files, but it does erase all files and data in memory. If the data in memory has not been saved to a disk, it is lost when the computer is rebooted. As warm booting the computer erases everything in memory, you should only warm boot your computer as a last resort if it is locked up and will not recognize any commands you enter.

To warm boot, [Ctrl] and [Alt] are held down while [Del] is pressed. (When two or more keys are pressed at the same time to enter a command, the keys are shown with a plus, such as [Ctrl]+[Alt]+[Del] for a warm boot.) Because the computer is already on, the self-diagnostic test is not performed. A warm boot takes less time than a cold boot to get the computer started and is not as hard on the computer as a cold boot.

To warm boot your computer:

1. With your floppy disk drive(s) empty, hold down [Ctrl] and [Alt] with your left hand while you press [Del] with your right hand. Release all three keys.

   Your computer will go through the same process of checking your floppy disk and hard drives for the operating system booting files as it did when you cold booted.

2. If your computer prompts you for the current date, press [Enter]

3. If your computer prompts you for the current time, press [Enter]

4. If your computer boots to display a menu, follow the instructions on the screen to exit to the DOS prompt.

Lesson 1/Computer Components and DOS

5. If your computer displays a Windows screen, press [Alt]+[F], type **x**, and press [Enter]

6. If your computer displays the DOS Shell, press [F3]

7. Type **cd ** and then press [Enter]

DATE AND TIME

Having your computer set for the correct date and time is important. When you save or change a file, your computer's date and time are stamped on the file. When you have several file revisions saved with similar names, you can look at a file's date and/or time to determine which filename was used for the latest revision.

To set your system's calendar:

1. Type **date** and press [Enter]. The screen displays a message showing the date used when the computer was booted. Although the message displays the day of the week, the day of the week is not entered when entering a new date to set the internal calendar.

2. Type **12-25-94** and press [Enter]. You just set the current date to December 25, 1994.

3. Type **date** and press [Enter]

4. Type **13-34-93** and press [Enter]. Your screen should look like Figure 1-4.

Figure 1-4
DATE error screen

```
C:\>DATE
Current date is Sun 12-25-94
Enter new date (mm-dd-yy): 13-34-93

Invalid date
Enter new date (mm-dd-yy): _
```

DOS is smart enough to recognize an invalid date such as 13 for the month or 34 for the day.

5. Type **9-10-95** and press [Enter]

6. Reenter the DATE command.

7. Enter today's date and press [Enter]

When entering the date, you can use a dash (-), slash (/), or a period (.) to separate the month, day, and year. When entering the year, you can either enter the last two digits or the entire year.

When TIME is entered from the DOS prompt, your system's current time is displayed. When the computer is booted, the internal clock is set to midnight (unless your computer has a battery-powered calendar/clock that keeps track of the date and time even when the computer is off).

When setting the time on the computer's internal clock, most users enter only the hour and the minute. However, the internal clock is set up so that the second and hundredth of a second can also be entered. When entering the time, you must type a colon (:) between the hour and minute.

Though the computer keeps time using a 24-hour clock, with DOS 6.0 you can use a P or p or add 12 to the hour to indicate P.M. For instance, to enter the time of 4:25 P.M. you can type 16:25, 4:25P, or 4:25p.

To set your system's clock:

1. Type **time** and press [Enter]. Your system's current time is displayed.

2. Type **9:15** and press [Enter]

3. Type **time** and press [Enter]

4. Type **10:77** and press [Enter]. Your screen should look like Figure 1-5.

Figure 1-5
TIME error screen

```
C:\>TIME
Current time is 9:15:41.16a
Enter new time: 10:77

Invalid time
Enter new time: _
```

DOS recognizes that 77 is an invalid minute number.

5. Type **7:30p** and press [Enter]

6. Reenter the TIME command.

7. Enter the current time and then press [Enter]

SPECIAL KEYS

If you have a printer hooked up to your computer, you can print a copy of every line of text currently on the screen by pressing [Print Screen]. (On some older computer models, you must hold down [Shift] when pressing [Print Screen].) A laser printer stores the screen image and waits to print until the page is full.

To print the current screen:

1. Turn on your printer. If you are using continuous feed paper, advance the paper so the perforation is just above the print head of the printer. If you are using single sheet paper, check to see that you have paper in the paper tray.

2. Press [Print Screen]. The text currently on the screen is printed.

3. If nothing happens and you are using single sheet paper, press the button by the on-line light and then press the Form Feed (FF) or Manual Feed button. After the sheet is printed, press the on-line button so the on-line light comes on again and the printer will be ready to print.

4. If nothing happens when you press [Print Screen] and your printer uses continuous feed paper, press [Shift]+[Print Screen].

You can also have the printer echo or mirror the monitor. Every line of text appearing on the screen is printed after control to the printer is activated. To have the printer echo the screen, press [Ctrl]+[Print Screen]. [Ctrl]+[Print Screen] is a toggle key that activates (print on) and deactivates (print off) the printer echo.

If you are using continuous feed paper, you should test that the printer echo is on by pressing [Enter]. If the echo is on, you should be able to see the paper advance one line and/or hear it print the DOS prompt. When you turn the printer echo off, press [Enter] to test that the echo is off. If you are using continuous feed paper, with the echo off you should not hear or see the printer advance.

To have the printer echo the screen:

1. Press [Ctrl]+[Print Screen]

> **CAUTION: Hold down [Ctrl] first, press [Print Screen], then let go of both keys. Holding [Ctrl]+[Print Screen] down too long activates and then deactivates control to the printer.**

2. Press [Enter]. With continuous feed paper you should see the printer advance one line as it prints the DOS prompt. If your printer uses single-sheet paper, it will be printed when the sheet is full.

3. Type **cd ** and press [Enter]

At times, when you enter a command, the results on the screen whiz by too fast to read. You can temporarily halt or suspend the execution of a command by pressing [Pause] or [Ctrl]+[S]. The display is temporarily interrupted or frozen until any key is pressed to continue.

To temporarily halt command execution:

1. Type **dir** and press [Enter]

2. Press [Ctrl]+[S] or [Pause]. Were you quick enough to temporarily halt the command execution? If not, try again.

3. Press any key to continue the command execution.

After you press [Enter] to execute a command, you might realize that you entered the wrong command. You can cancel a command's execution by pressing Ctrl+C or Ctrl+Break. A ^C appears on the screen to show the command was canceled. The caret (^) is DOS's shorthand to symbolize Ctrl.

To cancel a command:

1. Type **dir** and press Enter
2. Press Ctrl+C or Ctrl+Break. Were you quick enough to cancel execution of the command? If not, try again.

To turn off the printer echo:

1. Press Ctrl+Print Screen
2. With continuous feed paper, press Enter to test that the printer echo is off. You should not be able to hear the printer print or see the paper advance. If the printer echo is still on, press Ctrl+Print Screen and again test that the printer echo is off.
3. If your printer uses continuous feed paper, advance the paper so you can tear it off at the page perforation. If your printer uses single sheets, press the on-line button to take your printer off line and press the Form Feed or Manual Feed button.

To turn off your computer:

1. Turn off your printer, using the same switch or button you used to turn it on.
2. Turn off your computer, using the same switch you used to turn it on. If you turned on your monitor separately when you booted the computer, turn off your monitor, also using the same switch you used to turn it on.

■ SUMMARY OF COMMANDS

Topic or Feature	Command or Key	Page
Show the current drive	DOS prompt	4
Toggle between uppercase and lowercase letters	Caps Lock	5
Clear the screen	CLS	5
Enter special symbols on upper portion of keys	Shift	5
Toggle the numeric keypad between numbers and cursor movement	Num Lock	6
Restart (warm boot) the computer	Ctrl+Alt+Del	6
Change or display the current date	DATE	7
Change or display the current time	TIME	8

Topic or Feature	Command or Key	Page
Print information currently on the screen	[Print Screen] or [Shift]+[Print Screen]	8
Toggle the printer echo off and on	[Ctrl]+[Print Screen]	9
Interrupt the execution of a command	[Ctrl]+[S] or [Pause]	9
Cancel the execution of a command	[Ctrl]+[C] or [Ctrl]+[Break]	10

■ REVIEW QUESTIONS

1. The hard drive of a computer is referred to as drive _____.
2. Starting your computer when it is off is called a(n) _____ boot.
3. Restarting your computer when it is on is called a(n) _____ boot.
4. In order to type a symbol on the upper portion of a key, you must hold down _____ while pressing the key.
5. Both [Caps Lock] and [Num Lock] are examples of _____ keys.
6. To clear the screen, the command is _____.
7. When changing the system date, you (do/do not) _____ enter the day of the week.
8. To cancel the execution of a command, press ____+____.
9. The keys held down to warm boot the computer are ____+____+____.
10. To change or display the current system time, the command is _____.

■ HANDS-ON EXERCISES

Exercise 1-1   Turn on your computer and boot to the DOS prompt. Turn on the printer. Familiarize yourself with the keyboard by entering the TIME and DATE commands in uppercase, lowercase, and with only the first letter of each command capitalized.

Exercise 1-2   Warm boot the computer to the DOS prompt. Print the screen. Toggle on the printer echo and test that the echo is on. Type **dir** and press [Enter], and then temporarily halt execution of the command. Type **dir** and press [Enter], and then cancel the com-mand execution. Enter the command to clear the screen. Turn off the printer echo and test that the echo is off. Remove your printout. Turn off the printer, computer, and monitor.

LESSON TWO: DOS 6.0 Command Aids

OBJECTIVES

In this lesson you will learn how to:

- Display any temporary paths in memory.
- Enter a temporary path.
- Change the appearance of the DOS prompt.
- Display all commands for which FASTHELP is available.
- Display FASTHELP information for an individual command.
- Use DOSKEY to temporarily store commands in memory.
- Use DOSKEY recall commands.
- Use cursor movement keys to edit commands stored in memory.

DOS COMMANDS

DOS has two types of commands: internal and external. **Internal commands** are loaded into memory during the booting process and are available for execution whenever the computer is booted. The commands you learned in Lesson One (CLS, DATE, and TIME) are all internal commands.

As **external commands** are normally used less often than internal commands, they are stored on the hard disk drive. When you enter an external command, the computer must find the DOS file containing the command and load it into memory before it can be executed.

Just as drawers divide a filing cabinet to help organize papers, the hard disk on your computer is divided into directories to organize files. All disks have at least one directory—the **ROOT directory**. The ROOT directory, represented by the backslash symbol (\), was created when the disk was formatted (made ready to accept files).

The ROOT directory on the hard disk is normally divided into several directories to organize files. The files necessary to run your spreadsheet program are kept together in a directory. Another directory has the files needed to run your word-processing program. When DOS 6.0 was installed on your computer, all the files to execute external DOS commands were stored together in another directory. In order to execute external commands, you need to know the name of the directory where they are stored.

Lesson 2/DOS 6.0 Command Aids

To determine the directory where external commands are stored:

1. Boot your computer to the DOS prompt. (If necessary, follow the instructions on page 3 of Lesson One.)

2. Turn on your printer.

3. Type **cd ** and press (Enter)

4. If C:\>_ is not displayed as the DOS prompt, type **prompt pg** and press (Enter)

5. Type **dir /ad /p** and press (Enter). The /ad in the command you entered instructs DOS to list only the directories that divide the ROOT (\) directory. The /p tells DOS to pause if the screen is full.

6. Type **dir /ad > prn** and press (Enter). With > PRN added to the command, the list is printed instead of being displayed on the screen.

NOTE: You can add > PRN at the end of any command. Instead of displaying the action performed by the command on the screen, it is printed.

7. Remove your printout. If necessary, turn your printer on line again.

Look at your printout. All the names listed are directories as indicated by <DIR> to the right of the directory name. As the external commands are usually stored in a directory named DOS, look through the list and see if you have a directory named DOS.

If you do not have a directory named DOS on your printout, your external commands are stored in a directory with another name. Some alternative names that may have been used are DOS6, SYSTEM, DOSFILES, or OPSYS. Look at your printout to find the name of the directory in which the external DOS commands are stored. Use this directory name instead of DOS in commands you enter throughout this text.

To see all the DOS files for external commands:

1. Type **dir dos /on /p** and press (Enter). The /on sorts the filenames for the DOS external commands so they are listed in alphabetical order.

NOTE: If the external DOS commands are stored in a directory with a different name, use that name instead of DOS in the above command.

2. When the screen display halts, press any key to continue to view the files. Continue to press any key until you are back to the DOS prompt.

Look at the DOS prompt on your screen: C:\>_. The C: tells you that drive C is the current drive. The backslash (\) tells you that ROOT is the current directory. When you enter a command, it will be executed on the current directory of the disk in the current drive unless the command instructs otherwise.

The DOS files you displayed are stored on the current drive but not in the ROOT directory—they are stored in the DOS directory. The command you just entered (DIR DOS /ON /P) gave the name of the directory containing the files and instructed the computer to list the files alphabetically in the DOS directory. The DOS directory is one of the directories dividing the ROOT directory of your computer's hard disk.

PROMPT

The internal DOS command PROMPT changes the appearance of the DOS prompt. DOS 6.0 automatically changes the DOS prompt so it displays the current drive and directory after booting. However, your computer may be configured (set up) so that it only shows the drive and not the directory as part of the DOS prompt. As it is quite helpful to know which directory is the current directory, you can change your computer's DOS prompt so it also displays the current directory information by using the PROMPT PG command.

To change the DOS prompt:

1. Type **cd dos** and press [Enter]. The DOS prompt (C:\DOS>_) shows that the current drive is drive C and that the current directory is DOS. The backslash (\) shows that DOS is a division of the ROOT directory.

2. Type **prompt** and press [Enter]. You are still in the DOS directory, but the DOS prompt (C>_) only shows you the current drive.

3. Type **prompt pg** and press [Enter]. The DOS prompt now displays the current drive and directory.

NOTE: As you work with this text, if your DOS prompt does not display the current directory as part of the DOS prompt information, enter the command PROMPT PG after booting.

PATH

The internal DOS command PATH lets DOS know where to find the files to execute commonly used commands. For instance, with over 100 files listed in the DOS directory, it would be helpful if you could just enter the name of the file instead of having to remember that it is in the DOS directory.

DOS 6.0 automatically stores the path to the DOS directory in memory during booting. However, your computer may be configured (set up) so the path is removed.

To work with the PATH command:

1. Type **chkdsk** and press [Enter]. If you have a path to the DOS directory, in a few moments a status report about drive C is displayed. If the message "Bad command" is displayed, the path to the DOS directory was removed during booting.

2. If you received the error message "Bad command", type **path=c:\dos** and press [Enter]. The PATH command includes the drive (C:) and location (\DOS) of the directory.

3. Type **path** and press [Enter]. The message displays the directory path(s) in memory.

4. Type **chkdsk** and press [Enter]. DOS follows the directory path given in the PATH command and executes the external DOS command CHKDSK to display a status report about drive C.

5. Type **doskey** and press [Enter]. The message "DOSKey installed." is displayed on your screen. If the message is not displayed on your screen, press [F7]. Several commands are listed, showing that your computer is configured to load DOSKEY into memory during booting.

The PATH command is discussed more thoroughly in Lesson Ten.

NOTE: As you work with this text, you will frequently need to use the external DOS commands. If you needed to enter the path to the DOS directory in step 2, enter the command PATH=C:\DOS after booting.

FASTHELP

DOS 6.0 provides information to help users understand how to enter DOS commands. To view all the commands for which information is available from the command line, the command FASTHELP is entered.

To access information on commands:

1. Type **fasthelp** and press [Enter]. There is more information than can be displayed on one screen, so "---More---" is displayed at the bottom of the screen.

2. Press any key to continue the listing. Continue to view the listing until you are back at the DOS prompt.

You can also display the syntax (the way in which a command must be entered) for an individual command. To access information for an individual command, type the name of the command followed by /? or type **fasthelp** followed by the name of the command.

The slash (/) entered behind a command is referred to as a **switch**. The /? added behind a command is a switch used to access information on a command. Figure 2-1 displays the information for the DATE command.

Figure 2-1
DATE FASTHELP screen

```
C:\DOS>DATE /?
Displays or sets the date.

DATE [date]

Type DATE without parameters to display the current date setting and
a prompt for a new one.  Press ENTER to keep the same date.

C:\DOS>_
```

To access information for an individual command:

1. Type **date /?** and press Enter. The information displayed should be like that shown in Figure 2-1.

2. Type **fasthelp date** and press Enter. The same information is displayed for the DATE command.

3. Display the information available for the TIME command using the /? switch (**time /?**).

4. Display the information available for the CLS command without using the /? switch (**fasthelp cls**).

5. Display the information available for the PATH command using the /? switch (**path /?**).

DOSKEY

DOSKEY is a special external command that stores commands entered from the keyboard in a temporary storage area in memory. The commands are stored in a buffer and are available so you can edit (change or correct) and reuse them.

Most external commands, such as FASTHELP, need to be loaded into memory each time they are executed. Each time you enter FASTHELP, the FASTHELP.EXE file in the DOS directory must be loaded into memory before it can be executed. DOSKEY is a **terminate-and-stay-resident (TSR)** program. Unlike most external commands, once a TSR command is loaded into memory it is available until the computer is turned off or rebooted.

The keys used by DOSKEY to recall previously entered commands are listed in Table 2-1.

Lesson 2/DOS 6.0 Command Aids

Table 2-1   DOSKEY Recall Keys

Key	Function
↑	Scrolls forward through the commands one at a time.
↓	Scrolls backward through the commands one at a time.
Page Up	Displays the first command in the DOSKEY list.
Page Down	Displays the last command in the DOSKEY list.
F7	Displays all commands in a numbered DOSKEY list.
F8	Recalls the last command entered that began with the specified text.
F9	Prompts you to enter a command number from the numbered DOSKEY list displayed when F7 is used.
/history	Displays all commands in an unnumbered DOSKEY list. Type **doskey /history** and press Enter.

Once the command you want to reuse is displayed beside the DOS prompt, you can use the cursor movement to edit it or press Enter to execute it. Table 2-2 lists several of the keys frequently used to move the cursor when editing a command.

Table 2-2   DOSKEY Cursor Movement Keys

Key	Cursor Movement
←	Moves the cursor one character to the left.
→	Moves the cursor one character to the right.
Home	Moves the cursor to the beginning of the command line.
End	Moves the cursor to the end of the command line.
Del	Deletes the character the cursor is under.
Ins	Allows character(s) to be inserted at the cursor position. The cursor changes to a blinking rectangle when Ins is pressed.
Esc	Removes the displayed command from the DOS prompt.

DOSKEY is loaded into memory by typing **doskey** and then pressing Enter. As you loaded DOSKEY earlier in this lesson, the next activities have you practice using the recall keys and edit previously entered commands.

To use DOSKEY recall keys:

1. Clear the screen (**cls**).

2. Press Page Up. The first command entered after DOSKEY was installed is displayed.

3. Press Esc to remove the command from the DOS prompt.

4. Press [Page Down]. The last command entered (CLS) is displayed.
5. Remove the command from the DOS prompt by pressing [Esc].
6. Type **f** and then press [F8]. The last command entered starting with the letter f (FASTHELP CLS) is displayed. Remove the command.
7. Display the last command entered that started with T. (Type **t** and then press [F8].) The command TIME /? is displayed. Remove the command from the command line.
8. Press [F7]. All the commands you have entered since loading DOSKEY are displayed in a numbered list. Look at the number 4 command.
9. Press [F9]. In response to the prompt "Line number:" type **4** and press [Enter]. The fourth command is displayed. Press [Enter] to execute it.
10. Access the second command entered since DOSKEY was loaded into memory ([F9] **2**). Remove the command from the DOS prompt.
11. Type **doskey /history** and press [Enter]. All the commands are listed in an unnumbered list.

The cursor is a blinking rectangle when it is in **Insert mode**. In Insert mode, the characters you type are inserted at the cursor location and the previous text is moved to the right. In **Strikeover mode**, the cursor is a blinking underline. The characters you type replace the text at the cursor location. To toggle between Insert and Strikeover modes, press [Ins].

To edit previously entered commands:

1. Access the command FASTHELP CLS (type **f** and then press [F8] or press [↑] until it is displayed).
2. Edit the command to change it to CLS /?. (Press [End]. Type **/?** to add the /? switch. Press [Home]. Press [Del] nine times so that the C of CLS is the first character in the command. Press [Enter].)
3. Press [↑] until the command TIME /? is displayed.
4. Edit the command to change it to DATE /?. (Press [Home]. If necessary, change your cursor to Strikeover mode. Type **date**. The word DATE replaces TIME in the command displayed. Press [Enter] to execute the command.)
5. Display a numbered list of all the commands entered (press [F7]). Notice the number in front of the command PATH /?. Press [F9] and then type the line number for the PATH /? command. Press [Enter] to execute it.
6. Press [↑] to access the command PATH /? and change it to FASTHELP PATH. (Press [Home]. If necessary, change your cursor to Insert mode. Type **fasthelp** and press [Spacebar] once. Press [End]. Press [Backspace] to delete the /?.) Press [Enter] to execute it.
7. Access the command DOSKEY /HISTORY and execute it.

8. Access the last command entered. Type **> prn** and press [Enter] (**doskey /history > prn**) to print an unnumbered list of commands.

Now that you know how to use DOSKEY, you can use it to save a great deal of time by editing previously entered commands as you work through this text.

To remove your printout and turn off your computer system:

1. Remove your printout.
2. Turn off your printer, computer, and monitor.

■ SUMMARY OF COMMANDS

Topic or Feature	Command or Key	Page
Print the action performed by a command	> PRN	13
Change the DOS prompt to display the current drive and directory followed by >	PROMPT PG	14
Change the DOS prompt to only display the current drive followed by >	PROMPT	14
Display any current paths in memory	PATH	15
Enter a temporary path to the DOS directory on drive C into memory	PATH=C:\DOS	15
Display commands for which FASTHELP is available	FASTHELP	15
Display FASTHELP for an individual command	FASTHELP command name or command name /?	16
Load DOSKEY into memory	DOSKEY	17
Toggle cursor between Strikeover and Insert modes	[Ins]	18

■ REVIEW QUESTIONS

1. By adding _____ at the end of any command, the execution of the command is printed instead of being displayed on the monitor.

2. The two ways you can enter the command to access FASTHELP for the DATE command are _____ and _____.

3. With C:\>_ displayed as the DOS prompt, the current drive is drive _____ and the current directory is _____ .

4. The symbol used to represent the ROOT directory is the _____.

5. _____ DOS commands are available for execution when the computer is booted.

6. In order to execute _____ DOS commands, the computer must find the file containing the DOS command and load it into memory.

7. To enter a temporary path to the DOS directory on drive C into memory, the command is _____

8. To change the DOS prompt so it displays the current drive and directory followed by >, the command is _____.

9. A _____ program is an external command that once loaded into memory is available for use until the computer is turned off or rebooted.

10. Using DOSKEY, press _____ to display a numbered list of all commands entered since DOSKEY was loaded into memory.

■ HANDS-ON EXERCISES

Exercise 2-1 Boot your computer to the DOS prompt and turn on the printer. Display any current paths in memory. If necessary enter a temporary path to the DOS directory on drive C into memory. If necessary, change the DOS prompt to display the current drive and directory followed by >. Load DOSKEY. Display all the FASTHELP commands available. Display FASTHELP on the commands PROMPT, DOSKEY, DATE, PATH, CLS, TIME, and FASTHELP.

Exercise 2-2 Use the DOSKEY recall keys to recall and execute the following commands:

1. The first command in the DOSKEY list
2. The last command in the DOSKEY list
3. The last command entered that began with P
4. The fourth command entered
5. A numbered list of commands entered
6. An unnumbered list of commands entered

Access the last command entered and edit it to print an unnumbered list of commands entered. Remove your printout. Turn off your printer, computer, and monitor.

LESSON THREE
Disks and Drives

OBJECTIVES

In this lesson you will learn how to:

- Distinguish a double-density disk from a high-density disk.
- Handle and write protect a disk.
- Format a system and nonsystem disk to the drive capacity.
- Format a disk to double-density in a high-density drive.
- Change the current drive.
- List files on the current drive.
- Use the Directory (DIR) switches.
- List files on a target drive.

DISK DRIVES

Your computer has one or two disk drives for removable disks. If it only has one removable disk drive, the single drive is usually referred to as drive A. If your computer has two drives for removable disks side by side, usually the left drive is drive A and the right drive is drive B. If the drives for removable disks are stacked, the top drive is usually drive A and the bottom drive is usually drive B.

The drives for removable disks are available in different densities (double- or low-density, high-density, and extra-high-density). **Density** refers to how close together data is stored on a disk.

A drive is described by the number of **bytes** that it can read/write to a disk. A byte represents one character (a letter, number, space, or special symbol). PCs have two sizes of drives for removable disks: 3½-inch and 5¼-inch. Each size drive can only read or write to a disk of the same size. Table 3-1 lists the size and density of common PC drives for removable disks.

From looking at a drive, you can only tell its size—3½-inch or 5¼-inch; you cannot tell its capacity.

First Look at DOS 6.0

Table 3-1 Drive Sizes and Capacity

Size	Description	Capacity (bytes)
5¼-inch	Double-sided, double-density*	360KB**
3½-inch	Double-sided, double-density	720KB
5¼-inch	Double-sided, high-density	1.2MB***
3½-inch	Double-sided, high-density	1.44MB
3½-inch	Double-sided, extra-high-density	2.88MB

* Double-density is also called low-density
** KB: Kilobyte (kilo = 1,000 bytes)
*** MB: Megabyte (mega = 1,000,000 bytes)

Both sizes of floppy disks can be **write protected**. Write protection prevents the files from being accidentally erased, though the files can still be read (used) by DOS. The notch near the top of the upper-right side of the 5¼-inch disk is the write-protect notch. Covering the notch with a small, nontransparent adhesive tab write protects the disk. On the back side of a 3½-inch disk is a write-protect window. When the window is open, the disk is write protected. When the plastic slide is moved so the window is closed, the disk is no longer write protected.

The high-density 3½-inch disk has an added square cutout opposite the write-protect window to distinguish it from a double-density disk. It also usually has the letters HD stamped on it. The double-density 5¼-inch disk hub ring—the circle seen just inside the circular cutout in the middle of the disk—is darker than the rest of the disk surface. In addition, the manufacturer's label on the front top-left corner of the 5¼-inch disk should identify if the disk is double-density or high-density. Figure 3-1 shows the front and back sides of both the 3½-inch and 5¼-inch disks.

Figure 3-1
3½-inch and 5¼-inch disks

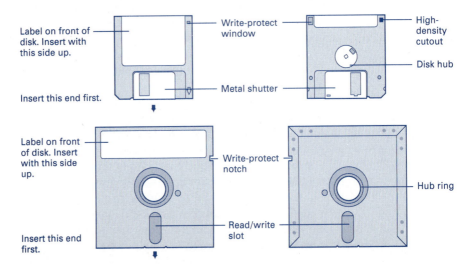

When you buy a floppy disk, it should come with a self-adhesive paper label, used to identify the contents of the disk. Use only a felt-tip pen to write on a label once you have put it on the disk. The 5¼-inch floppy disk should also come with a small adhesive tab for write protection and a paper jacket.

The floppy disk surface is coated with iron oxide for magnetization and requires care in handling. Avoid exposing your disks to magnetic fields such as those emitted from the phone or stereo. As the read/write slot exposes part of the 5¼-inch disk surface, keep the disk in its paper jacket, be careful not to touch the exposed area, and store it so it will not be bent. To preserve the life of your disks, avoid prolonged exposure of them to direct sunlight or extreme cold.

FORMAT

Because disks can be used with many different microcomputers with different operating systems, a disk must be customized to be recognized by your operating system. The external DOS command FORMAT is used to prepare a disk so that you can use it with your computer system. During the formatting process, DOS sets up a **file allocation table** (**FAT**) where it keeps track of the locations of each file stored on the disk.

A disk can be formatted as a **system disk** or a **nonsystem disk**. A system disk is able to boot your computer; a nonsystem disk is not able to boot your computer. A system disk contains the special DOS files in the ROOT directory. Two of the booting system files, IO.SYS and MSDOS.SYS, handle input/output requests. The third booting system file, COMMAND.COM, loads the internal DOS commands into memory so they are available for execution. The fourth booting system file, DBLSPACE.BIN, enables the system disk to work with disk drives whose files have been compressed.

If your computer has high-density drives, you should buy high-density disks. You can format a high-density disk to either high-density or double-density. You should avoid, however, formatting a double-density disk to high-density as the disk was not manufactured to be able to store data as closely packed together as it is on a high-density disk.

> *CAUTION: The FORMAT command erases a disk. If a disk that already contains data is formatted again, all files on it are erased.*

To boot your computer:

1. Boot your computer to the DOS prompt.

2. If necessary, enter a temporary path to the DOS directory on drive C into memory (**path=c:\dos**) and change the DOS prompt so it displays

the current drive and directory followed by > (**prompt pg**). Load DOSKEY (**doskey**).

To format a disk:

1. Insert your new blank disk into drive A:

   a. With a 3½-inch disk, insert the end with the metal slide into the drive first with the metal hub down and label up (horizontal drive) or the metal hub on the side of the drive having a small button (vertical drive).

   b. With a 5¼-inch disk, insert the end with the oval read/write slot into the drive first with the write-protect notch on the left (horizontal drive) or the write-protect notch on the bottom (vertical drive). Close the drive door.

NOTE: *The 5¼-inch disk drives have a drive door that must be closed by turning a lever or pulling a door to position the disk.*

2. Type **format a:** and press Enter. Without any switches added to the FORMAT command, the disk is formatted to the drive capacity. To format a disk in drive B, you would type **B:** instead of A:.

NOTE: *When a disk drive is entered as part of a command, the letter of the drive must be followed by a colon.*

3. The following message appears on the screen:

```
Insert new disk for drive A:
and press ENTER when ready...
```

CAUTION: Carefully read the message. If the drive in the message is not the drive in which you inserted your disk, cancel the command (press Ctrl+C) and then reenter it.

4. As your disk is already in drive A, press Enter after checking the displayed message.

CAUTION: Never open or close a drive door to insert or remove a disk while the drive light is on. If you do, you risk not only ruining your disk, but also your disk drive.

The formatting process takes several seconds. A message on the screen tells you the percentage of the disk formatted. When the disk is formatted, the following message appears on the screen:

```
Format complete.
Volume label (11 characters, ENTER for none)? _
```

DOS is waiting for you to give an internal name to the disk.

5. Type your first name and press [Enter]

After displaying information about the space available on your newly formatted disk and its serial number, another message appears on the screen:

```
Format another (Y/N)?_
```

6. Type **n** and press [Enter]. You are returned to the DOS prompt.

7. Look at the format information about the space available on your newly formatted disk. Refer to Table 3-1 on page 22 to determine whether drive A on your computer is a double-density, high-density, or extra-high-density drive.

8. Type **dir a:** and press [Enter]. The information about the disk in drive A should be similar to Figure 3-2.

Figure 3-2
Directory of newly formatted disk

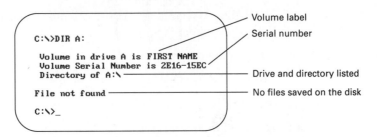

The third line, Directory of A:\, tells you the drive (A:) and the directory (\) being listed. As there are no files on the disk, the message "File not found" is displayed.

The disk you just formatted is a nonsystem disk. It does not contain the special files DOS needs in order to boot the computer. To format a system disk, the /S switch is added to the FORMAT command.

To format a system disk:

1. Enter the command **format a: /s** and press [Enter]
2. As your disk is still in drive A and you are reformatting it, press [Enter] in response to the message telling you to insert a new disk in drive A.
3. As your disk was previously formatted, DOS displays the messages:

```
Checking existing disk format.
Saving UNFORMAT information
```

4. After the disk is formatted, type your last name in response to the prompt requesting you to enter a volume label and press [Enter]
5. Type **n** and press [Enter] in response to the message asking whether you want to format another disk.
6. Look at the format information telling you about the space available on your disk. The system booting files used over 180KB of disk space.
7. Type **dir a:** and press [Enter]. Instead of the message "File not found", the file COMMAND.COM is listed. The next two lines tell you the number of files listed, the number of bytes in the listed file(s), and the number of bytes available on your disk.
8. Type **dir a: /ah** and press [Enter]. The hidden booting files IO.SYS, MSDOS.SYS, and DBLSPACE.BIN are listed. Files on your disks can be compressed to almost double disk storage capacity with DOS 6.0. When you boot your computer with your floppy disk, the DBLSPACE.BIN file enables your system to work with the compressed drive.
9. Type **dir a: /as** and press [Enter]. The hidden booting files listed in step 8 are also system files.
10. Turn on the printer.
11. Print the screen ([Print Screen] or [Shift]+[Print Screen]).

As your disk is a system disk, it can be used to boot the computer.

To warm boot your computer:

1. Warm boot your computer ([Ctrl]+[Alt]+[Del]).
2. If requested, enter the current date and time. The DOS prompt is A:\>_ showing that drive A is the current drive.
3. Type **path** and press [Enter]. When you boot from a floppy disk, the DOS prompt is changed to show the current drive and directory, but the path to the DOS directory is not loaded into memory. The message "No Path" is displayed.

4. Enter a temporary path to the DOS directory on drive C into memory (**path=c:\dos**). Load DOSKEY (**doskey**).

CHANGE THE CURRENT DRIVE

Since you booted your computer from your disk in drive A, drive A is the current drive. By looking at the DOS prompt, you can readily tell the current drive. To change the current drive, type the desired drive letter followed by a colon.

To change the current drive:

1. Type **c:** and press [Enter] to change the current drive to drive C.
2. Type **a:** and press [Enter] to change the current drive to drive A.
3. Change the current drive to drive C (**c:**).

FORMAT DOUBLE-DENSITY DISKS IN HIGH-DENSITY DRIVES

The use of high-density disk drives is increasing. A high-density disk drive can read or write to a double-density formatted disk. A double-density disk drive cannot read or write to a high-density formatted disk.

A disk can be formatted as double-density in a high-density drive by using the /F switch with the FORMAT command. FORMAT A: /F:360 formats a 5¼-inch disk to double-density. FORMAT A: /F:720 formats a 3½-inch disk to double-density. The /S switch can be added to both of these commands to format a system disk.

DIR (DIRECTORY)

The DIR (Directory) command is one of the most frequently used internal DOS commands. It is used to display the names of files saved on a disk. Figure 3-3 shows a screen listing for the DIR command.

The vertical file listing displays five columns of information about each file listed. You can see the name of the file, the extension of a filename, the file size, and the file date and time stamp. If the filename listed is a directory name, <DIR> is listed between the extension column and the file size column.

Figure 3-3
DIR listing

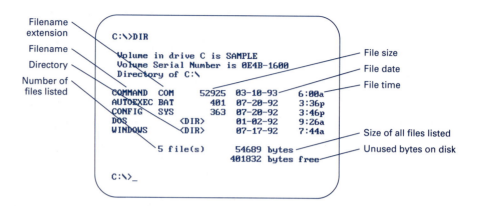

DIR Switches

Two of the most commonly used DIR switches are the /P switch and the /W switch. The /P switch pauses the directory listing when the screen is full; the /W switch displays a wide or columnar listing of files. Both the /P and /W switches are also available in prior DOS versions.

To use the DIR command and the /W and /P switches:

1. Type **dir /w** and press [Enter]. The names of files and directories are displayed in five columns on the screen with the directory names enclosed in square brackets. The size, date, and time information is not listed.

2. Type **cd dos** and press [Enter]. The DOS prompt should be C:\DOS>_.

3. Type **dir /p** and press [Enter]. When the screen is full, the message "Press any key to continue..." is displayed. Press any key and continue to view the file listing until you are back to the DOS prompt.

DOS 6.0 has several switches that can be used with the DIR command. Figure 3-4 shows the FASTHELP information for the DIR command.

To use DIR switches:

1. Display the FASTHELP information for the DIR command (**dir /?**). The information displayed should be the same as Figure 3-4.

2. Type **dir /on /p** and press [Enter]. The directory is listed in order of the filename. Continue to press any key when the listing pauses until you are back to the DOS prompt.

3. Type **dir /oe /p** and press [Enter]. The files are listed in order by the filename extension.

4. Do a wide directory listing sorted by extension (**dir /oe /w**).

Figure 3-4
DIR FASTHELP information

```
C:\>DIR /?

Displays a list of files and subdirectories in a directory.

DIR [drive:][path][filename] [/P] [/W] [/A[[:]attribs]] [/O[[:]sortord]]
    [/S] [/B] [/L] [/C[H]]

  [drive:][path][filename]  Specifies drive, directory, and/or files to list.
  /P        Pauses after each screenful of information.
  /W        Uses wide list format.
  /A        Displays files with specified attributes.
  attribs   D  Directories    R  Read-only files      H  Hidden files
            S  System files   A  Files ready to archive  -  Prefix meaning "not"
  /O        List by files in sorted order.
  sortord   N  By name (alphabetic)       S  By size (smallest first)
            E  By extension (alphabetic)  D  By date & time (earliest first)
            G  Group directories first    -  Prefix to reverse order
            C  By compression ratio (smallest first)
  /S        Displays files in specified directory and all subdirectories.
  /B        Uses bare format (no heading information or summary).
  /L        Uses lowercase.
  /C[H]     Displays file compression ratio; /CH uses host allocation unit size.

Switches may be preset in the DIRCMD environment variable.  Override
preset switches by prefixing any switch with - (hyphen)--for example, /-W.

C:\>_
```

5. Type **cd ** and press Enter. The DOS prompt should be C:\>_.

6. List the files sorted by date (**dir /od**).

7. List the hidden files (**dir /ah**).

8. List the system files (**dir /as**).

9. List the directories (**dir /ad**).

List Files on a Target Drive

To list the files on another drive, you can change the current drive or include the **target drive** as part of the DIR command. A target drive is any drive other than the current drive. For instance, if drive C is the current drive and you want to list the files on drive A, drive A is the target drive (the one on which the command is to be performed).

To do a directory listing of the target drive:

1. Type **dir a:** and press Enter. Drive A is the target drive.

2. Change the current drive to drive A (**a:**).

3. Type **dir c: /w** and press Enter. The files in the target drive (drive C) are listed in columns.

4. Type **dir c: /p** and press Enter. The files on drive C are listed with the display temporarily halted when the screen is full.

5. List the hidden files sorted by size on drive C **(dir c: /ah /os)**.

6. Do a wide directory listing of directories sorted in order by name on drive C **(dir c: /ad /on /w)**.

To turn off your system:

1. Advance the paper in the printer and remove your printout.

2. Remove your disk from drive A. Push the small button on the 3½-inch drive. Your disk will pop out so that you can remove it. With a 5¼-inch disk, use the same lever or handle to open the drive door as you used to close the drive door.

3. Write ACTIVITY and your name on the paper label to identify your disk. If the paper label is already affixed to your disk, use a felt-tip pen. Activities throughout the rest of this text will refer to this disk as the ACTIVITY disk.

4. Turn off the printer. Turn off your computer and monitor.

■ SUMMARY OF COMMANDS

Topic or Feature	Command or Key	Page
Format a nonsystem disk in drive A	FORMAT A:	24
Format a system disk in drive A	FORMAT A: /S	26
Format a 3½-inch high-density disk to double-density	FORMAT A: /F:720	27
Format a 5¼-inch high-density disk to double-density	FORMAT A: /F:360	27
Change the current drive to drive A	A:	27
Change the current drive to drive C	C:	27
List the names of files	DIR	27
Display a wide listing of files	DIR /W	28
Display a listing of files that pauses when the screen is full	DIR /P	28
Display a listing of files sorted by the filename	DIR /ON	28
Display a listing of files sorted by the extension	DIR /OE	28

Topic or Feature	Command or Key	Page
Display a listing of files sorted by date	DIR /OD	29
Display a listing of files sorted by size	DIR /OS	30
Display a listing of hidden files	DIR /AH	29
Display a listing of system files	DIR /AS	29
Display a listing of directories	DIR /AD	29
Display a listing of files on drive C (target drive)	DIR C:	29

■ REVIEW QUESTIONS

1. A (system/nonsystem) _____ disk must be used to boot your computer.

2. FORMAT is an (internal/external) _____ DOS command.

3. To format a system disk in drive A the command is _____.

4. To format a 3½-inch high-density disk in drive A as a system disk in double-density, the command is _____.

5. A kilobyte (KB) represents a (thousand/million) _____ bytes.

6. A megabyte (MB) represents a (thousand/million) _____ bytes.

7. The command to display a listing of files on the current drive is _____.

8. With drive A as the current drive, the command to display a listing of files on drive C (the target drive) is _____.

9. With drive A as the current drive, type _____ to change the current drive to drive C.

10. Use a _____ when writing on a paper label already affixed to a disk.

■ HANDS-ON EXERCISES

Exercise 3-1 Boot your computer to the DOS prompt from the hard drive. Turn on the printer. If necessary, enter a temporary path to the DOS directory on drive C into memory and change the DOS prompt so it displays the current drive and directory followed by >. Load DOSKEY. Insert your ACTIVITY disk into drive

A and format it as a nonsystem disk with your first name as a volume label. Print the screen. Format your ACTIVITY disk in drive A as a system disk with your last name as a volume label. Print the screen.

Exercise 3-2

Activate control to the printer and test that the printer is echoing the screen. Do the following directory listings on the current drive:

1. A wide listing
2. A listing sorted by the filename
3. A listing that pauses when the screen is full
4. A wide listing sorted by the extension
5. A listing sorted by date
6. A listing of the hidden files

Change the current drive to drive A. Perform the six directory listings on drive C (target drive). Display an unnumbered list of commands entered since loading DOSKEY.

Deactivate control to the printer and test that the printer is not echoing the screen. Remove your printout. Turn off the printer, computer, and monitor. Remove your ACTIVITY disk.

LESSON FOUR: Multidirectory Disks

OBJECTIVES

In this lesson you will learn how to:

- Use filenames and extensions.
- Use the DOS wild-card characters.
- Use directories to help manage files.
- View the directory structure of a disk.
- View the directory structure and the files in each directory of a disk.
- Change the current directory.
- Determine the current directory.
- Make subdirectories.
- Remove subdirectories.

FILENAMES AND EXTENSIONS

Filenames identify specific files with which DOS is to work. The file might be an application program, a data file used by an application program, or a DOS file. A filename is made up of two parts: the **name** and an optional **extension**. Each file stored in a directory must have a unique filename. However, the same filename and extension can be used on different disks or in different directories on the same disk.

A filename can be from one to eight characters in length. The maximum length of an extension is three characters. If an extension is listed with the filename, then it usually must be used in a command when referring to that file. DOS uses a period to separate the filename and the extension. Valid filename characters are:

- Uppercase letters (A–Z)
- Lowercase letters (a–z)
- Numbers (0–9)
- Special symbols ! @ # $ % ^ & ( ) _ - { } ~ ` '

The special symbols * + = [ ] ¦ : ; " , . / \ < > ? and blank spaces are invalid filename characters. Table 4-1 lists several filenames with an explanation of why the filename is valid or invalid.

Table 4-1 Valid and Invalid Filenames

Filename	Valid or Invalid	Explanation
CHTEST	Valid	An extension is optional.
CHTEST12.ABC	Valid	Numbers are valid filename characters.
CH TEST.ABC	Invalid	Spaces are not allowed in filenames.
CHTEST .ABC	Invalid	Do not leave a space before or after the period separator.
ch1-2.abc	Valid	DOS is not case-sensitive; a hyphen is a valid filename character.
CHAPTEST.ABC3	Invalid	Maximum extension length is three characters.
CHAPTEST1.ABC	Invalid	Maximum filename length is eight characters.

WILD-CARD CHARACTERS

DOS has two wild-card characters that enable you to selectively work with files. The asterisk (*) represents several characters in a filename or extension; the question mark (?) represents one character in a filename or extension. DIR is one of several DOS commands with which the wild-card characters are used.

To boot your computer:

1. Boot your computer from the hard disk to the DOS prompt.
2. If necessary, enter a temporary path to the DOS directory on drive C into memory and change the DOS prompt so it displays the current drive and directory followed by >. Load DOSKEY.

To practice using the wild-card characters:

1. Type **cd dos** and press [Enter]. The DOS prompt should be C:\DOS>_.
2. Type **dir *.sys** and press [Enter] to list only the files with a SYS extension. The asterisk (*) indicates that any characters can make up the name of the file.

3. Type **dir s*.exe** and press [Enter] to list only files starting with the letter S that have an EXE extension. After starting with S, any characters can make up the rest of the filename.

4. Type **dir d*.*** and press [Enter]. Only files starting with the letter D are listed. Any characters can make up the rest of the filename and the extension.

5. Type **dir mo?e.*** and press [Enter] to list all four-letter files with any extension that start with the letters MO and end with E. The question mark (?) indicates that any one character can be the third character.

6. Type **dir *er.sys** and press [Enter]. As soon as DOS reads an asterisk in a filename or extension, it ignores any other characters you enter. All the files listed have a SYS extension, but all the filenames do not have ER as the last characters.

7. Type **dir ?a*.*** and press [Enter] to list all files with the letter A as the second filename character.

MULTIPLE DIRECTORIES

Setting up multiple directories on a disk is like using a large filing cabinet that has several drawers. Each drawer can have many file folders separated by dividers to aid in organizing files.

Because of the tremendous amount of storage space on disks, they can be divided into several directories to help you organize your files. Organizing files saved on a hard disk into multiple directories is not a luxury—it is a necessity. Application programs like Lotus, WordPerfect, and Windows each should be saved on the hard disk in a separate directory. The data files created and used with each application program should also be saved in separate directories. Figure 4-1 illustrates a sample multidirectory disk structure.

Both floppy and hard disks can be set up with multiple directories. ROOT (\) is the initial or primary directory of every disk created during formatting. A multilevel directory structure is created through repeated divisions of

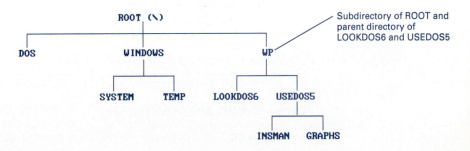

Figure 4-1
Sample multi-directory disk structure

directories. In Figure 4-1, the ROOT directory is divided into three directories—DOS, WINDOWS, and WP. The WINDOWS and WP directories are both further divided into directories. The USEDOS5 directory is again divided into additional directories.

A division of a directory is a **subdirectory.** A directory and subdirectory are the same; "sub" means it is a division of a directory. In Figure 4-1, DOS, WINDOWS, and WP are subdirectories of the ROOT directory. LOOKDOS6 and USEDOS5 are subdirectories of WP. INSMAN and GRAPHS are both subdirectories of USEDOS5.

A **parent directory** is a directory that has been divided. ROOT is the parent directory of DOS, WINDOWS, and WP. WINDOWS is the parent directory of SYSTEM and TEMP. WP is the parent directory of LOOKDOS6 and USEDOS5. USEDOS5 is the parent directory of INSMAN and GRAPHS.

A directory can be both a subdirectory and a parent directory. In Figure 4-1, WINDOWS is a subdirectory of ROOT and a parent directory to SYSTEM and TEMP; WP and USEDOS5 are also both subdirectories and parent directories.

TREE

The external DOS command TREE is used to view the directory structure of a disk. The TREE command lists the directory structure vertically. Figure 4-2 shows the same multidirectory structure as Figure 4-1, using the TREE command. The vertical and horizontal lines show the subdirectories of each directory.

Figure 4-2
Sample TREE listing of a multidirectory disk structure

```
C:\>TREE
Directory PATH listing for Volume SAMPLE
Volume Serial Number is 0E4B-1600

C:.
├──DOS
├──WINDOWS
│   ├──SYSTEM
│   └──TEMP
└──WP
    ├──LOOKDOS6
    └──USEDOS5
        ├──INSMAN
        └──GRAPHS

C:\>_
```

To view a disk's directory structure:

1. Type **cd ** and press [Enter]. The DOS prompt should be C:\>_.

2. Type **tree** and press [Enter]. The entire directory structure of your hard drive is displayed.

3. Change the current drive to drive A (**a:**).

4. Type **tree c:** and press [Enter] to display the directory structure of drive C.

5. Change the current drive to drive C (**c:**)

Directory Names

Directory names follow the same naming conventions as filenames, discussed earlier in this lesson. Usually a directory name is short, such as WP for a directory containing your word-processing program, or DB for the directory in which your database program is saved. The directory name should be descriptive enough to enable you to recognize the type of files stored in it.

CD (CURRENT DIRECTORY/CHANGE DIRECTORY)

Current Directory

A current directory is where DOS expects to find the file(s) specified in a command. The disk in each drive has a current directory. The CD command is used to determine the current directory. When CD is used, the entire directory path starting with the drive and the ROOT directory is displayed.

To determine the current directory:

1. Type **prompt** and press [Enter] so the DOS prompt does not display the name of the current directory.

2. Type **cd dos** and press [Enter]

3. Type **cd** and press [Enter]. C:\DOS is displayed. The \ starts the directory path at the ROOT directory. As DOS is listed behind the backslash, you can tell that DOS is a subdirectory of ROOT. As no directory names are listed after DOS, DOS is the current directory.

4. Type **cd a:** and press [Enter]. A:\ is displayed on the screen showing that ROOT is the current directory on drive A.

5. Change the current drive to drive A.

6. Determine the current directory on drive C (**cd c:**).

7. Change the current drive to drive C.

8. Determine the current directory on drive C. The DOS directory on drive C is still the current directory.

9. Change the DOS prompt so it displays the current drive and directory followed by >.

The steps you just completed illustrated two concepts: changing the current drive does not change the current directory, and you do not have to change the current drive to determine the current directory on another drive.

Change Directory

Besides determining the current directory, the CD command is also used to change the current directory. The command CD \ instructs DOS to change the current directory to the ROOT (\) directory. With drive A as the current drive, CD C:\ changes the current directory on drive C (the target drive) to ROOT. If you want to change the current directory to a subdirectory, enter the directory name after the CD command. The command CD DOS changes the current directory from the ROOT directory to the DOS subdirectory. After making several directories on your ACTIVITY disk later in this lesson, you will learn more about using the CD command.

To change the current directory:

1. Type **cd ** and press [Enter] to change the current directory on drive C to the ROOT directory.

2. Type **cd dos** and press [Enter] to change the current directory on drive C from the ROOT directory to the DOS directory.

3. Change the current drive to drive A.

4. Determine the current directory on drive C (**cd c:**).

5. Change the current directory on drive C to the ROOT directory (**cd c:**).

6. Determine the current directory on drive C (**cd c:**).

MD (MAKE A DIRECTORY)

The MD command is used to make or create a directory. The syntax of the MD command is the same as that of the CD command you used to change the current directory. The command MD SPSHEET makes SPSHEET as a subdirectory to the current directory.

To make a directory:

1. With drive A as the current drive, type **md sports** and press Enter. You just created SPORTS as a subdirectory of the ROOT directory.

2. Type **dir** and press Enter. After the COMMAND.COM file, SPORTS is listed with <DIR> on the same line to tell you that SPORTS is a subdirectory.

3. Make the directory TRAVEL (**md travel**).

4. Do a directory listing. Both SPORTS and TRAVEL are listed as subdirectories of the ROOT directory.

5. Change the current directory to SPORTS (**cd sports**).

6. Make the directory SOCCER (**md soccer**).

7. Make the directory GOLF (**md golf**).

8. Do a directory listing. SOCCER and GOLF are listed as subdirectories of SPORTS. Your directory listing should be similar to Figure 4-3.

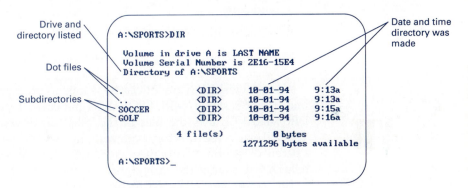

Figure 4-3
Directory listing of a subdirectory

When a new directory is created, a single dot (.) and a double dot (..) are the first two directory entries. DOS uses the single dot to refer to the current directory and the double dot to refer to the parent directory. The date and time displayed are the current date and time when the directories were created.

The third line in the heading information, A:\SPORTS, tells you the drive and directory listed. The backslash in front of SPORTS indicates that SPORTS is a subdirectory of ROOT.

You can execute commands on a subdirectory by entering the subdirectory name after the command. From a subdirectory you can execute commands on the parent directory by using the **double dot (..) command**.

To practice working with directories:

1. Change the current directory to SOCCER (**cd soccer**).

2. Do a directory listing (**dir**). The third line in the heading, A:\SPORTS\SOCCER, shows that SPORTS is a subdirectory of ROOT and SOCCER

is a subdirectory of SPORTS. Multiple directory names are separated by a backslash (\).

3. Type **dir ..** and press (Enter) to list the parent directory (SPORTS) files.
4. Type **dir** and press (Enter) to list the ROOT directory files.
5. Type **cd ..** and press (Enter) to change the current directory to the parent directory (SPORTS).
6. Type **dir soccer** and press (Enter) to do a directory listing of the SOCCER subdirectory.
7. Change the current directory to SOCCER (**cd soccer**).
8. Type **cd ** and press (Enter) to change the current directory to ROOT.
9. Change the current directory to TRAVEL (**cd travel**).
10. Make EUROPE as a subdirectory to the current directory, TRAVEL (**md europe**).
11. Do a directory listing. After the two dot files, EUROPE is listed as a subdirectory.
12. Change the current directory to ROOT.
13. Display the directory structure of your ACTIVITY disk (**tree**).

You can work with any directory as long as your command tells where to find it. For instance, with SPORTS as the current directory, the command DIR \TRAVEL lists the files in the TRAVEL directory. The \ in front of TRAVEL starts the directory path with the ROOT directory as TRAVEL is not a parent or subdirectory of the current directory. The command CD \TRAVEL tells DOS to change the current directory to TRAVEL.

The command DIR \TRAVEL\EUROPE does a directory listing of EUROPE. The directory path starts at the ROOT directory. As EUROPE is a subdirectory of TRAVEL, a backslash is used between directory names. The command CD \TRAVEL\EUROPE changes the current directory to EUROPE.

To continue working with directories:

1. Change the current directory to SPORTS (**cd sports**).
2. Do a directory listing of TRAVEL (**dir \travel**).
3. Do a directory listing of EUROPE (**dir \travel\europe**).
4. Change the current directory to TRAVEL (**cd \travel**).
5. Do a directory listing of SPORTS.
6. Do a directory listing of SOCCER (a subdirectory of SPORTS).
7. Do a directory listing of GOLF (a subdirectory of SPORTS).

To display the directory structure:

1. Display the directory structure of your ACTIVITY disk (**tree**).

NOTE: DOS 6.0 starts the directory structure listing with the current directory. With TRAVEL as the current directory, only the subdirectory EUROPE is listed.

2. Change the current directory to ROOT.

3. Display the directory structure of your disk. As ROOT is the current directory, the entire directory structure is displayed.

The TREE command has a /F switch that is used to list the files in each directory while displaying the directory structure.

To display the directory structure and files:

1. Type **tree /f** and press [Enter]. COMMAND.COM in the ROOT directory is the only file on your ACTIVITY disk. You can tell that COMMAND.COM is a file as it does not have a vertical or horizontal line used to indicate a subdirectory.

2. Change the current drive to drive C.

3. Type **tree a: /f** and press [Enter] to list the directory structure and files on drive A.

4. Change the current drive to drive A.

RD (REMOVE A DIRECTORY)

The RD command is used to remove an empty subdirectory. It can only contain the two dot files. You cannot remove the current directory. The RD command syntax is the same as that of the CD and MD commands. To remove a directory, the RD command must give the path to the directory to be removed.

To remove a directory:

1. Change the current directory to SPORTS (**cd sports**) and do a directory listing.

2. Type **rd soccer** and press [Enter] to remove the SOCCER subdirectory.

3. Do a directory listing. The two dot files and the GOLF subdirectory are listed.

4. Change the current directory to GOLF (**cd golf**).

5. Type **rd golf** and press [Enter]. As GOLF is the current directory, the following error message is displayed:

> ```
> Invalid path, not directory,
> or directory not empty
> ```

6. Change the current directory to ROOT (**cd **).

7. Type **rd travel** and press Enter. As the TRAVEL directory is not empty (it still has the subdirectory EUROPE), the same error message is displayed.

8. Remove the EUROPE subdirectory of TRAVEL (**rd travel\europe**).

DELTREE

Instead of having to remove directories one at a time, the DELTREE command of DOS 6.0 will remove a directory and all of its subdirectories and files.

NOTE: Use the DELTREE command with caution so you do not accidentally delete a subdirectory containing files you need to keep.

To use DELTREE to remove several directories:

1. Display the directory structure of your disk (**tree**).

2. Type **deltree sports** and press Enter. The following message is displayed:

> ```
> Delete directory "sports" and all its subdirectories? [yn]_
> ```

3. Type **y** and press Enter. You just removed the SPORTS directory and its subdirectory GOLF.

4. Display the directory structure of your disk.

5. Remove the TRAVEL directory (**deltree travel**).

6. Display the directory structure of your disk. No subdirectories are listed.

7. Do a directory listing. Only the COMMAND.COM file is listed.

Working with multidirectory structured disks is a very common DOS activity. The remaining lessons will continue to work with multiple directories. If you feel unsure of yourself when working with multiple directories, you may want to reread and rework through this lesson before doing the Hands-On Exercises.

To turn off your computer:

1. Turn off your computer and monitor.
2. Remove your ACTIVITY disk from drive A.

■ SUMMARY OF COMMANDS

Topic or Feature	Command or Key	Page
Use wild-card characters to:		
Replace one character in a filename or extension	?	34
Replace several characters in a filename or extension	*	34
Display the directory structure of the current drive	TREE	36
Display the directory structure of drive A (target drive)	TREE A:	37
Display the directory structure and files on the current drive	TREE /F	41
Display the current directory on the current drive	CD	37
Display the current directory on drive A (target drive)	CD A:	37
Change the current directory to a subdirectory	CD directory name	38
Change the current directory to the ROOT directory	CD \	38
Change the current directory on drive C (target drive) to the ROOT directory	CD C:\	38
Make a subdirectory	MD directory name	39
Change the current directory to the parent directory	CD ..	40
Remove a subdirectory	RD directory name	41
Remove a directory and its subdirectories and files	DELTREE directory name	42

44 First Look at DOS 6.0

■ REVIEW QUESTIONS

1. The primary directory of any disk is the _____ directory, which is symbolized by the backslash (\) symbol.

2. A _____ directory is a directory that has been divided; a _____ is a division of a directory.

3. The command _____ displays the directory structure of a disk.

4. To list the files in the parent directory, the command is _____.

5. With drive A as the current drive, to display the name of the current directory on drive C the command is _____.

6. To make TRAVEL as a subdirectory of the current directory, the command is _____.

7. With \WORDPRO\BUSINESS as the current directory, to change the current directory to ROOT the command is _____.

8. TEMP is a subdirectory of the current directory. The command to change the current directory to TEMP is _____.

9. With ROOT as the current directory, to remove TRAVEL (subdirectory of ROOT) and all its subdirectories enter the command _____.

10. The command _____ changes the current directory to the parent directory.

■ HANDS-ON EXERCISES

Exercise 4-1

Boot your computer from the hard disk. Turn on the printer. Activate control to the printer so it echoes the screen and test that the echo is on. If necessary, enter a temporary path to the DOS directory on drive C and change the DOS prompt so it displays the current drive and directory followed by >. Load DOSKEY. Insert your ACTIVITY disk into drive A.

Change the current directory to the DOS directory. Do the following directory (DIR) listings of the DOS directory:

   1. Files starting with the letter D

   2. Files with an EXE extension

3. All four-letter files with O as the second letter—any characters can make up the extension

Change the current drive to drive A. Perform the three directory listings with drive C as the target drive.

Exercise 4-2

Drive A should still be the current drive. Create the following directories:

1. LESSON as a subdirectory of ROOT

2. EXERCISE as a subdirectory of LESSON

3. TESTDIR as a subdirectory of ROOT

4. PRACTICE as a subdirectory of TESTDIR

With ROOT as the current directory, display the directory structure of your ACTIVITY disk. Change the current directory to PRACTICE. Do a directory listing of the following directories:

1. TESTDIR

2. ROOT

3. LESSON

Change the current directory to TESTDIR. Do a directory listing of the following directories:

1. PRACTICE

2. ROOT

3. LESSON

Use the RD command to remove the PRACTICE directory. Change the current directory to ROOT. Display the directory structure of your ACTIVITY disk. Remove the TESTDIR directory. Remove the LESSON and EXERCISE directories in one command. Do a directory listing.

Display an unnumbered list of commands that have been entered since DOSKEY was loaded into memory. Deactivate control to the printer and test that the echo is off. Remove your printout. Turn off the printer, computer, and monitor. Remove your disk.

LESSON FIVE: File Management

OBJECTIVES

In this lesson you will learn how to:

- Use the DOS wild-card characters with several commands.
- Copy files.
- Move files.
- Rename files.
- Use EDIT to create a file.
- Display the contents of a file.
- Erase files.
- Undelete a deleted file.

COPY

The purpose of the COPY command is to copy files. In order to copy, the command must let DOS know where the original file(s) is located (source) and where the file(s) is to be copied (destination). You can use either or both of the DOS wild-card characters (* and ?) to copy several files in one command. You will copy some of the files in the DOS directory on drive C to your ACTIVITY disk in drive A.

To boot your computer:

1. Boot your computer to the DOS prompt from the hard drive.
2. If necessary, enter a temporary path to the DOS directory on drive C and change the DOS prompt so it displays the current drive and directory followed by >. Load DOSKEY.
3. Insert your ACTIVITY disk into drive A.
4. Turn on the printer.
5. Format your ACTIVITY disk in drive A as a nonsystem disk. When requested, enter your last name as the volume label **(format a:)**.
6. Change the current drive to drive A.

7. Make the following directories on your ACTIVITY disk:

   WORDPRO as a subdirectory of ROOT

   BUSINESS as a subdirectory of WORDPRO

   TRAVEL as a subdirectory of ROOT

   CLASS as a subdirectory of ROOT

   NOTES as a subdirectory of CLASS

8. With ROOT as the current directory on drive A, display the directory structure of your ACTIVITY disk. The directory structure should be the same as that shown in Figure 5-1.

Figure 5-1
ACTIVITY disk directory structure

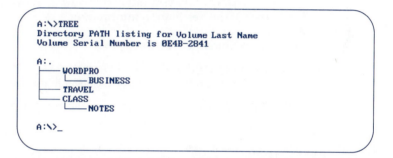

To copy from the current drive to a target drive:

1. Change the current drive to drive C.

2. Change the current directory on drive C to DOS (**cd dos**).

3. Determine the current directory on drive A. (**cd a:**). The current directory should be ROOT. If not, type **cd a:** and press [Enter]

4. Type **copy c:ega.sys a:** and then press [Enter]. The source of EGA.SYS is the current directory on drive C and the destination is the current directory on drive A. After the file is copied, the message "1 file(s) copied" is displayed.

5. Copy the file MORE.COM from the current directory on drive C to the current directory on drive A.

6. Type **copy c:f*.* a:** and then press [Enter] to copy all the files starting with the letter F in the current directory on drive C to the current directory on drive A. As each file is copied, the name of the file is displayed. After the copy process is complete, the number of files copied is listed.

7. Copy all files beginning with L in the current directory on drive C to the current directory on drive A.

To copy from the target drive to the current drive:

1. Change the current drive to drive A. ROOT should be the current directory.
2. Type **copy c:edit.com a:** and press [Enter]. The source of EDIT.COM is the current directory on drive C and the destination is the current directory on drive A.
3. Copy HELP.COM from the current directory on drive C to the current directory on drive A.
4. Type **copy c:?h*.exe a:** and then press [Enter]. The files with an EXE extension with H as the second filename character are copied from the current directory on drive C to the current directory on drive A.

When copying a file, you can give it a new name. The new name is specified as part of the destination information.

To change a filename while copying:

1. Type **copy c:l*.* a:x*.*** and then press [Enter]. As the files are copied, DOS changes the names to begin with the letter X instead of L.
2. Copy all files starting with L in the current directory on drive C and change the extension to XYZ in the current directory on drive A **(copy c:l*.* a:*.xyz)**.
3. Do a directory listing that pauses when the screen is full. After the WORDPRO, TRAVEL, and CLASS subdirectories are listed, the files copied to the ROOT directory are listed.

The previous activities copied files from one disk to another disk. The next activities have you copy files to different directories on your ACTIVITY disk. If you omit either the source or destination from the COPY command, DOS assumes it is to use the current drive and directory.

To copy files to another directory on the same disk:

1. Type **copy edit.com travel** and press [Enter]. The source of EDIT.COM is the current drive and directory (A:\). The destination is the TRAVEL subdirectory of ROOT on drive A.

    The command can be entered as **copy a:\edit.com a:\travel** to give the entire source and destination directory paths. As the source of EDIT.COM is the current drive and directory and the destination is a subdirectory of the current directory on the current drive, there is no need to include the drive and start the destination from ROOT when entering the command.

2. Copy EDIT.COM in the current directory to WORDPRO (a subdirectory of ROOT) **(copy edit.com wordpro)**.
3. Copy files beginning with L in the ROOT directory on drive A to TRAVEL (a subdirectory of ROOT) **(copy l*.* travel)**.

4. Type **copy help.com wordpro\business** and press Enter. The source of HELP.COM is the current directory on drive A. The destination is WORDPRO\BUSINESS on the current drive.

5. Copy files with an XYZ extension from the current drive and directory to the BUSINESS subdirectory of WORDPRO (**copy *.xyz wordpro\business**).

6. Type **copy l*.* wordpro\z*.*** and press Enter. All files starting with L in the current directory on drive A (source) are copied to WORDPRO (destination). During the copy process, the files are renamed to start with Z in the WORDPRO directory. A backslash separates the directory name from the filename.

7. Copy HELP.COM from the current directory on drive A to WORDPRO with the name AID.EXE (**copy help.com wordpro\aid.exe**).

8. Change the current directory to BUSINESS (subdirectory of WORDPRO) (**cd wordpro\business**).

9. Copy all the files in the current directory to the CLASS (subdirectory of ROOT) directory (**copy *.* \class**).

10. Change the current directory to ROOT.

11. Display the directory structure and files on your disk (**tree /f**).

12. Print the directory structure and files on your disk (**tree /f > prn**).

MOVE

What if you realize that you copied a file to the wrong directory? With DOS 6.0 you can move the file to the correct directory. In effect, the MOVE command copies the file to the destination directory and then erases it from the source directory. As with the COPY command, DOS must know where the original file(s) is (source) and where the file(s) is to be moved (destination). Like the COPY command, you can use either or both of the DOS wildcard characters (* and ?) to move several files in one command.

To move a file:

1. Change the current directory to CLASS.

2. Type **move help.com notes** and press Enter to move the file from the current directory to the subdirectory NOTES. DOS verifies the file was moved by displaying the following message:

```
a:\class\help.com => a:\class\notes\help.com [ok]
```

3. Change the current directory to ROOT.

4. Do a directory listing of all files starting with the letter F.

5. Move all the files starting with the letter F in the ROOT directory to the NOTES directory (**move f*.* class\notes**). A message is displayed verifying each file you moved.

6. Do a directory listing of all files starting with the letter F. None are listed as you just moved them to the NOTES directory.

7. Change the current directory to NOTES (**cd class\notes**).

8. Copy the files starting with FA in the current directory to the ROOT directory (**copy fa*.* **).

9. Change the current directory to ROOT.

REN (RENAME)

You do not have to copy a file in order to give it a different name. You can rename a file with the internal DOS command REN (Rename).

NOTE: When renaming a file using the REN command, you do not specify a directory path or drive for the renamed file.

To rename files in the current directory:

1. With ROOT as the current directory, type **ren ega.sys *.abc** and press [Enter] to rename the file from EGA.SYS to EGA.ABC. As the renamed file is to have the same filename, the * is used for the filename. Alternately, you could enter the command as **ren ega.sys ega.abc**. Unlike the COPY command, the REN command does not list the files being renamed or show how many files are renamed.

2. Rename LABEL.EXE to TAG.EXE (**ren label.exe tag.***). As the renamed file is to have the same extension, the * can be used for the extension. Alternately, you could enter the command as **ren label.exe tag.exe**.

3. Change the current directory to WORDPRO.

4. Do a directory listing.

5. Rename AID.EXE to AID.TXT (**ren aid.exe *.txt**). As the filename is not changed, use an asterisk instead of typing it.

6. Do a directory listing of files with a COM extension (**dir *.com**).

7. Rename files with a COM extension to EXE as the extension (**ren *.com *.exe**). Just the extensions, not the filenames, are changed.

8. Do a directory listing of files with an EXE extension. Three files are listed.
9. Rename all files with an EXE extension to a TXT extension (**ren *.exe *.txt**).
10. Change the current directory to ROOT on drive A.

EDIT

EDIT, an external DOS command, is a DOS text editor that allows you to create a file. Figure 5-2 shows the EDIT screen when creating a file. The menu bar displays names of available drop-down menus from which commands are selected. The lower right-hand corner displays the line and position of the cursor. You can use either a mouse or the keyboard to move the cursor and select commands in EDIT (working with a mouse is covered in later lessons).

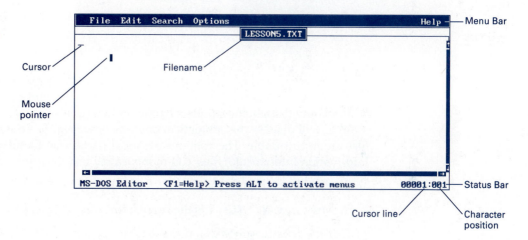

Figure 5-2
EDIT screen

To create a file using EDIT:

1. Type **edit a:\lesson5.txt** and press [Enter] to instruct EDIT to work with a file named LESSON5.TXT in the ROOT directory on drive A.

As you do not have a file named LESSON5.TXT in the ROOT directory on drive A, a blank screen like Figure 5-2 appears when EDIT is loaded so you can create the file. The name of the file, LESSON5.TXT, is centered near the top of the screen. The cursor position is 00001:001 (line 1, position 1). The cursor is blinking in the top-left corner.

2. Type the following, pressing [Enter] at the end of each line. (Type the requested information for the lines in parentheses.)

**(your first name and last name)
EDIT is a limited word processor that works with ASCII files.**

ASCII file contents are readable when displayed on the screen. (today's date)

3. To save your file and exit EDIT:

   a. Press [Alt]+[F]. All Menu Bar items can be accessed by pressing [Alt] while typing the first letter of the item. The File drop-down menu appears. One letter in each command listed in the drop-down menu is in a different color.

   b. Type **s** (the letter in a different color for the **S**ave command in the drop-down menu) to execute **S**ave. Your file is saved to your ACTIVITY disk in drive A.

   c. Press [Alt]+[F].

   d. Type **x** to execute Exit. EDIT is exited and you are returned to the DOS prompt.

TYPE

The TYPE command is used to display the contents of a file. TYPE is one of the few DOS commands with which you *cannot* use the wild-card characters. You can only display the contents of one file at a time.

TYPE will display the contents of any file; however, the contents of some files are not readable. The contents of ASCII (American Standard Code for Information Interchange) files, commonly called text files, are readable.

To display the contents of a file:

1. Make sure that ROOT is the current directory on drive A.

2. Type **type lesson5.txt** and press [Enter]. This is the file you just created using EDIT. EDIT files are automatically saved as ASCII or text files. The contents are readable when viewed on the screen.

3. Display the contents of EGA.ABC (**type ega.abc**). Your computer beeps a couple of times and lots of different symbols are displayed. As this is not an ASCII file, the contents are not readable when displayed on the screen.

DEL (DELETE)

As you use the computer more and more, over a period of time you have files saved on your disks that you no longer need or want. To remove the unwanted files and give yourself more room on the disks, files can be erased using the internal DOS command DEL (Delete). Like the COPY and REN commands, you can use the wild-card characters to erase multiple files with one command.

As a precaution when erasing one or several files, you should do a directory listing of the file(s) to be erased to make sure they are the right file(s). Then edit the command to change the DIR to DEL.

To erase files in the current directory:

1. Drive A should be the current drive. Change the current directory to WORDPRO.

2. Type **dir aid.txt** and press [Enter]. The one file is listed.

3. Edit the last command to change DIR to DEL. (Display the original command by pressing [↑]; then press [Home] and type **del** so the command is del aid.txt). Press [Enter]. The file is erased. DOS does not display any message indicating that the file is erased.

4. Change the current directory to BUSINESS (subdirectory of current directory).

5. Do a directory listing to list the file HELP.COM (**dir help.com**).

6. Delete the file HELP.COM (**del help.com**).

7. Change the current directory to the ROOT directory.

8. Do a directory listing of the file HELP.COM and then delete it.

To erase multiple files:

1. Do a directory listing of files with A as the second letter in the current directory (**dir ?a*.***).

As you look at the listing, you realize that you do not want to erase all of the files listed. You just want to erase the files starting with FA.

2. Edit the last command to erase just the files starting with FA (**del fa*.***).

To erase all the files in a directory:

1. Change the current directory to WORDPRO (subdirectory of ROOT).

2. Do a listing of the files in the current directory.

3. Type **del *.*** and press [Enter]. Erasing all the files in a directory is a drastic move. When you use *.* in the DEL command, DOS checks that this really is the action you want to take by displaying:

```
All files in directory will be deleted!
Are you sure (Y/N)?_
```

4. Look at the DOS prompt. Double-check that the current drive is drive A and that WORDPRO is the current directory. Double-check that the command entered is del *.*.

CAUTION: *If the command is DEL C:*.* you would erase all the files in the current directory on drive C! If the command is DEL *.* you would erase all the files in the ROOT directory on the current drive.*

    5. Type **y** and press [Enter]

In Lesson Four, you learned to use the RD command to remove a directory and the DELTREE command to remove a directory and its subdirectories in one command. What if the directory to be removed has files? To use the RD command, the directory to be removed cannot have any files. The DELTREE command erases the files while removing the directory.

To erase files and remove a directory:

1. Change the current directory to ROOT on drive A.
2. Display the directory structure and files on the current drive.
3. Change the current directory to CLASS (**cd class**).
4. Do a listing of files in the NOTES subdirectory (**dir notes**).
5. Try to remove the NOTES subdirectory using the RD command (**rd notes**).

    The error message explains why you cannot remove NOTES.

6. Erase all the files in the NOTES directory (**del notes*.***).
7. Now remove the NOTES subdirectory (**rd notes**).
8. Do a directory listing. The subdirectory NOTES is not listed.
9. Change the current directory to ROOT.
10. Remove the CLASS directory and its files in one command (**deltree class**).
11. Do a directory listing. CLASS is no longer listed.

UNDELETE

DOS 6.0 offers you several levels of protection against the accidental deletion of files—Delete Sentry, Delete Tracker, and Standard. Both the Delete Sentry and Delete Tracker levels use 13.5KB of memory for the memory-resident portion of the UNDELETE program.

The highest level of protection, Delete Sentry, creates a hidden directory to which it moves the deleted files. Delete Tracker provides an intermediate level of protection by allowing you to specify the number of deleted files that it should track. When you boot your computer, the Standard level of protection is automatically available. Your computer may be configured to install either Delete Sentry or Delete Tracker during booting.

The best time to undelete a file is immediately after it has been deleted. Unless you are using the Delete Sentry level of protection, if other files are copied to the same disk before you try to undelete, your effort will probably be unsuccessful. Figure 5-3 shows deleting a file and the screen messages and prompts to undelete the file with the Standard level of undelete protection.

Figure 5-3
UNDELETE screen

To delete and undelete a file:

1. With ROOT as the current directory on drive A, do a directory listing of the file EGA.ABC.

2. Delete the file EGA.ABC (**del ega.abc**).

3. Type **undelete ega.abc** and press [Enter] to undelete the file. The screen messages should be similar to Figure 5-3.

4. Type **y** when prompted with "Undelete (Y/N)?"

5. Type **e** when prompted for the first character of the filename.

6. Do a directory listing of files beginning with E. The file EGA.ABC should be listed.

7. If the file is not listed, type **undelete ega.abc /dos** as your computer was set up to use a higher level of protection. After the file is undeleted, do a directory listing of files beginning with E. The file EGA.ABC is listed.

To turn off your computer:

1. Advance the paper in your printer and remove your printout.

2. Turn off the printer, computer, and monitor. Remove your disk.

■ SUMMARY OF COMMANDS

Topic or Feature	Command or Key	Page
Copy file from current directory on drive C (source) to the current directory on drive A (destination)	COPY C:filename.ext A:	47
Copy file with a different name	COPY C:filename.ext A:newname.ext	48
Copy file to subdirectory	COPY filename.ext directory name	48
Copy file to the ROOT directory	COPY filename.ext \	50
Move file to subdirectory	MOVE filename.ext directory name	49
Move file to the ROOT directory	MOVE filename.ext \	50
Rename file in current directory	REN filename.ext newname.ext	50
Use EDIT to create a file in the ROOT directory on drive A	EDIT A:\filename.ext	51
Save a file in EDIT	File |Save	52
Exit EDIT	File |Exit	52
Display the contents of a text file	TYPE filename.ext	52
Erase file in current directory	DEL filename.ext	53
Erase all files in current directory	DEL *.*	53
Undelete an erased file	UNDELETE filename.ext	55

■ REVIEW QUESTIONS

1. To copy OLD.TXT in the current directory on drive C to the current directory on drive A, the command is _____.

2. To copy OLD.TXT in the current directory on drive C to the current directory on drive A with the name NEW.TXT, the command is _____.

3. To move OLD.TXT in the current directory on drive A to PRACTICE (subdirectory of current directory on drive A), the command is _____.

4. To load EDIT to create a file named NEW.TXT in the ROOT directory on drive A, the command is _____.

5. To save a file in EDIT, press _____ and then type _____.
6. To display the contents of the file NEW.TXT in the current directory, the command is _____.
7. To rename the file OLD.TXT to NEW.TXT, the command is _____.
8. To erase the file BUDGET.WP in the current directory, the command is _____.
9. To erase all the files in the current directory, the command is _____.
10. If a file is accidentally deleted, the _____ command is used to undelete it.

■ HANDS-ON EXERCISES

Exercise 5-1

Boot your computer from the hard drive to the DOS prompt. Turn on the printer. If necessary, enter a path to the DOS directory on drive C and change the DOS prompt so it displays the current drive and directory followed by >. Load DOSKEY. Insert your ACTIVITY disk into drive A. Change the current drive to drive A. Type **edit a:\prac.txt** and press [Enter] to create the file PRAC.TXT in the ROOT directory on drive A. Press [Enter] after typing each of the following lines. (Type the requested information for the lines in parentheses.)

(first and last name)
(current date)
This is an ASCII file created
using EDIT while doing the
Hands-On Exercises for Lesson Five.

Save the file and exit EDIT. Activate control to the printer so that it echoes the screen. Test that the echo is on.

Exercise 5-2

With ROOT as the current directory on drive A, do the following:

1. Copy PRAC.TXT to the subdirectory TRAVEL.
2. Display the contents of PRAC.TXT.
3. Rename PRAC.TXT to PRACTICE.TXT.
4. Change the current directory to TRAVEL.

5. Delete the file PRAC.TXT.
6. Undelete the file PRAC.TXT.
7. Move the file PRAC.TXT to the ROOT directory.
8. Change the current directory to ROOT.
9. Display the directory structure and files of your ACTIVITY disk.
10. Display an unnumbered list of commands entered since DOSKEY was loaded into memory.

Deactivate control to the printer. Test that the echo is off. Remove your printout. Turn off the printer, computer, and monitor. Remove your disk.

Disk Management

OBJECTIVES

In this lesson you will learn how to:

- Duplicate a floppy disk.
- Copy a disk's directory structure and files to a different-sized disk.
- Check the integrity of file structures.
- Check a disk for file fragmentation.
- Optimize a disk by defragmenting its files.
- Transfer the system booting programs.

DISKCOPY

When you buy an application program, the manual usually suggests that you make a copy of the disks before using the program. This is the time to use the external DOS command DISKCOPY. DISKCOPY can only be used to duplicate a floppy disk to another floppy disk of the same size and density. You cannot duplicate a double-density disk to a high-density disk. Figure 6-1 illustrates the screen when copying a 3½-inch high-density disk with one floppy disk drive. DISKCOPY works best if you have two floppy disk drives of the same size and density; otherwise, you are continually switching disks.

To boot your computer:

1. Boot your computer from the hard drive to the DOS prompt. Perform the normal startup activities (path to DOS directory, change the DOS prompt, and load DOSKEY).

To duplicate your ACTIVITY disk:

1. Insert your ACTIVITY disk into drive A.

   a. Type **diskcopy a: a:** and press Enter

   b. The screen prompts you to insert your source (original) disk into drive A. As you already have the source ACTIVITY disk in drive A, press any key.

Figure 6-1
DISKCOPY screen

```
C:\>DISKCOPY A: A:

Insert SOURCE diskette in drive A:

Press any key to continue . . .

Copying 80 tracks
18 Sectors/Track, 2 side(s)

Insert TARGET diskette in drive A:

Press any key to continue . . .

Formatting while copying

Insert SOURCE diskette in drive A:

Press any key to continue . . .

Insert TARGET diskette in drive A:

Press any key to continue . . .

Volume Serial Number is 0FEA-433B

Copy another diskette (Y/N)?N

C:\>_
```

    c. In a few moments the screen will prompt you to insert your target disk into drive A.

    d. Remove your ACTIVITY disk, insert a blank disk into drive A, and press any key.

    e. As the blank disk is not formatted, the screen displays a message that it is formatting while copying.

    f. Continue to follow the screen instructions to switch disks.

2. When your disk is duplicated, type **n** and press ⟨Enter⟩ in response to the message asking if you want to copy another disk.

3. Do a wide directory listing of your disk in drive A (**dir a: /w**).

4. Remove your duplicated disk; insert your ACTIVITY disk into drive A.

5. Do a wide directory listing.

6. Write NUMONE on the paper label before affixing it to your duplicate disk.

XCOPY

XCOPY is a special external DOS command that not only copies files, but also the directory structure of a disk to a different-sized disk. XCOPY is more versatile than DISKCOPY. For instance, you can copy the files and directory structure of a 5¼-inch disk to a 3½-inch disk or the hard drive. XCOPY has several switches that let you selectively copy files.

To use XCOPY:

1. Change the current drive to drive A. ROOT should be the current directory.

2. Display the FASTHELP information available for the XCOPY command (**xcopy /?**).

3. Type **xcopy a:\ c:\act /s /e** and press Enter

    This command copies your ACTIVITY disk starting at the ROOT directory (A:\) to the ROOT directory of drive C (C:\) and creates a new directory called ACT. The /S switch indicates that all subdirectories of the current directory are also to be copied. The /E switch indicates that even subdirectories that are empty are to be copied.

    After entering the command, the message shown in Figure 6-2 appears on the screen. The message is checking whether ACT is a directory or a file.

Figure 6-2
XCOPY screen

```
A:\>XCOPY A:\ C:\ACT /S /E

Does ACT specify a file name
or a directory name on the target
(F = file, D = directory)? _
```

4. Type **d** to indicate that ACT is a directory.

    As the files are copied, the entire directory path for each file copied is displayed on the screen. After the copy process is complete, the message tells you how many files were copied.

5. Change the current drive to drive C.

6. Change the current directory on drive C to ACT (**cd act**).

To view the copied directory structure and files:

1. Turn on the printer.

2. Print the directory structure and files (**tree /f > prn**).

3. Print the directory structure and files on your ACTIVITY disk in drive A (**tree a:\ /f > prn**).

4. Advance the paper in the printer and remove your printout. You will see that the files and directory structure on your ACTIVITY disk in drive A are the same as the files and directory structure beginning with the ACT directory on drive C.

The XCOPY command is very versatile. It can be used to copy an entire disk structure and files as in the last activity. You can also use XCOPY to selectively copy files.

To selectively copy files:

1. Insert your NUMONE disk into drive A.

2. Change the current directory on drive A to TRAVEL (**cd a:travel**).

3. Do a directory listing of drive A.

4. Type **xcopy c: a: /d:1-1-94** and press [Enter]

    This command instructs DOS to copy files from the current directory on drive C (**c:**) to the current directory on drive A (**a:**) that have a date of January 1, 1994, or later (**/d:1-1-94**). The files you created in Lesson Five using EDIT are copied to the current directory on drive A. All the other files are dated earlier than 1-1-94.

5. Do a directory listing of drive A. The files copied are among the files listed in the TRAVEL directory.

6. Type **xcopy c: a: /s** to copy the current directory and all subdirectories on drive C to the current directory on drive A.

7. Change the current directory on drive A to ROOT (**cd a:**).

8. Display the directory structure of drive A (**tree a:**).

9. If necessary, change the current drive to drive C.

CHKDSK (CHECK DISK)

CHKDSK is an external DOS command that checks the integrity of file structures on a disk. It analyzes the files, directories, and the file allocation table (FAT) to produce a status report of a disk and the computer memory. Figure 6-3 shows the CHKDSK status report when a high-density 3½-inch disk was checked. The report shows that the floppy disk has some bad, or unusable, sectors.

To check a disk:

1. Type **chkdsk** and press [Enter]. A status report of your hard drive is displayed.

2. Type **chkdsk a:** and press [Enter] to display a status report on your NUMONE disk in drive A.

When DOS writes a file to a disk, it writes the file in the first available area. If the area is not large enough to hold the entire file, DOS writes as much of

Figure 6-3
The CHKDSK screen

```
A:\>CHKDSK

Volume LAST NAME    created 10-01-1994 9:02a
Volume Serial Number is 2E16-15EC

  1457664 bytes total disk space
    72192 bytes in 3 hidden files
     1536 bytes in 3 directories
   221696 bytes in 24 user files
     9216 bytes in bad sectors
  1152024 bytes available on disk

      512 bytes in each allocation unit
     2847 total allocation units on disk
     2252 available allocation units on disk

   655360 total bytes memory
   594720 bytes free

A:\>_
```

the file as possible and then looks for the next available area to continue writing the file. If a file has a lot of activity (deletions, revisions), it may become fragmented as parts of the file are recorded in several noncontiguous (not adjacent) areas. Fragmented files slow down a computer's performance as it takes longer to read the file into memory and write the file to the disk.

To determine file fragmentation:

1. Type **chkdsk *.*** and press [Enter]. The fragmented files in the current directory on drive C are listed at the bottom of the status report.

2. Type **chkdsk a:*.*** and press [Enter] to check drive A for fragmented files in the current directory.

DEFRAG (DEFRAGMENT)

The DEFRAG command analyzes file fragmentation on a disk and reorganizes the files to optimize a disk's read/write performance time. The DEFRAG command physically rewrites a disk's files so that the files are written in contiguous areas.

To defragment a disk's files:

1. Type **defrag a:** and press [Enter]. An optimization report similar to Figure 6-4 is displayed. The Optimize button is highlighted.

2. If the optimization report shows that no optimization is necessary, press [Enter] and then type **x** to exit DEFRAG.

3. Press [Enter] to begin the optimization of your NUMONE disk in drive A. When the optimization is complete, a dialog box telling you that DOS has finished condensing is displayed.

Figure 6-4
DEFRAG screen for disk optimization

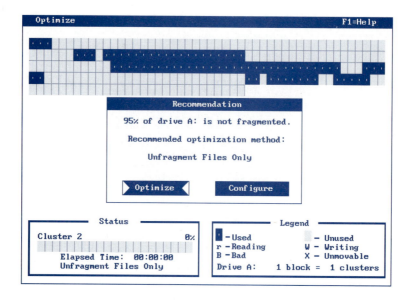

4. Press [Enter] to accept the message.

5. Another dialog box checks whether you wish to optimize another drive.

6. Press your [→] twice to highlight "Exit DEFRAG" and press [Enter]

7. Check your NUMONE disk again for file fragmentation (**chkdsk a:*.***).The status report shows that all files are in contiguous (adjacent) areas.

8. Change the current drive to drive A. ROOT should be the current directory.

9. Display the directory structure.

10. Delete the TRAVEL directory and all its subdirectories (**deltree travel**).

11. Change the current drive to drive C.

SYS (SYSTEM)

When you format a disk, you can add the /S switch to format the disk as a system disk. If you do not add the /S switch and later decide that you need to be able to boot the computer with your disk, you can use the external SYS command to make any formatted disk a system disk.

In order to use the SYS command, the current drive must be a system disk and DOS must be able to access the booting files in the ROOT directory and the external SYS command in the DOS directory.

Lesson 6/Disk Management

To create a system disk:

1. Make sure that drive C is the current drive with ROOT as the current directory.
2. Type **path=c:\dos;c:** and press [Enter] to enter a path to the DOS and ROOT directories on drive C.
3. Your NUMONE disk is in drive A. Check that ROOT is the current directory on drive A (**cd a:**). If necessary, change the current directory on drive A to the ROOT directory (**cd a:**).
4. Type **sys a:** and press [Enter]. The booting files are copied to the ROOT directory on drive A.

   DOS displays the message:

   ```
   System transferred
   ```

5. Warm boot your computer with your NUMONE disk in drive A. As the booting files were transferred to your disk, it is now a system disk that can be used to boot the computer.

To turn off your computer:

1. Turn off your computer and monitor.
2. Remove your NUMONE disk.

■ SUMMARY OF COMMANDS

Topic or Feature	Command or Key	Page
Make a duplicate floppy disk using one disk drive	DISKCOPY A: A:	59
Copy all files and directories (even empty) on drive A to a directory created on the hard drive	XCOPY A:\ C:\directory name /S /E	61
Copy files in the current directory that were created or changed after a given date to drive A	XCOPY C: A: /D:mm-dd-yy (month-day-year)	62
Copy files in the current directory and subdirectories to the current directory on drive A	XCOPY C: A: /S	62

Topic or Feature	Command or Key	Page
Check the disk in the current drive	CHKDSK	62
Check the disk in drive A (target drive)	CHKDSK A:	62
Check a disk for file fragmentation	CHKDSK *.*	63
Check the disk in drive A (target drive) for file fragmentation	CHKDSK A: *.*	63
Optimize drive A (target drive) disk's performance by reorganizing the files	DEFRAG A:	63
Copy the system booting programs to the disk in drive A	SYS A:	65

■ REVIEW QUESTIONS

1. Using the DISKCOPY command, you (can/cannot) _____ copy a floppy disk to the hard drive.

2. Using the DISKCOPY command, you (can/cannot) _____ copy a 5¼-inch floppy disk to a 3½-inch floppy disk.

3. Using the XCOPY command, you (can/cannot) _____ copy a 5¼-inch floppy disk to a 3½-inch floppy disk.

4. To create the directory PRACTICE off the ROOT directory on drive C while copying all the files and directory structure of a floppy disk in drive A, the command is _____.

5. The _____ switch is used in the XCOPY command to indicate all subdirectories.

6. The _____ command checks the integrity of files, directories, and the file allocation table (FAT).

7. To check for file fragmentation on the disk in drive A, the command is _____.

8. A file is _____ when it is not written in contiguous areas on a disk.

9. To optimize the performance of the disk in drive A by reorganizing the files, the command is _____.

10. To transfer the system booting files to the disk in drive A, enter the command _____.

■ HANDS-ON EXERCISES

Exercise 6-1 With your NUMONE disk in drive A, boot your computer. Turn on the printer. Enter a temporary path to the DOS and ROOT directories on drive C (**path=c:\dos;c:**) and load DOSKEY. Activate the printer echo. Test that the printer is echoing your screen. Remove your NUMONE disk and insert your ACTIVITY disk into drive A.
    Duplicate your ACTIVITY disk to your NUMONE disk. With ROOT as the current directory on drive A, display the directory structure and files of your NUMONE disk.

Exercise 6-2 Insert your ACTIVITY disk into drive A. Change the current drive to drive C with ROOT as the current directory. Transfer the system booting files to your disk in drive A. Change the current directory on drive C to WORDPRO (subdirectory of ACT). Copy the current directory and all subdirectories (even empty) to drive A while making the directory LESSON6.

Exercise 6-3 Change the current drive to drive A with ROOT as the current directory. Display the directory structure and files on your disk. Check your disk for file fragmentation. Optimize your disk in drive A by defragmenting it. Display an unnumbered list of commands entered since loading DOSKEY. Deactivate the printer echo. Test that the printer echo is off. Remove your printout. Turn off your equipment and remove your disk.

LESSON SEVEN
DOS 6.0 Shell

OBJECTIVES

In this lesson you will learn how to:

- Access and exit the DOS Shell.
- Identify the parts of the DOS Shell.
- Use the mouse and keyboard when working with the DOS Shell.
- Open and close drop-down menus.
- Use the Scroll Bars.
- Access HELP.
- Expand and collapse a Directory Tree.
- Selectively list files.

DOS SHELL BASICS

DOS 6.0 provides two ways in which you can enter most commands—via the keyboard or through the DOS Shell. This lesson is designed to acquaint you with the basics of the DOS 6.0 Shell.

Identifying Parts of the DOS Shell

The different parts of the DOS Shell window are identified in Figure 7-1. It is important to be familiar with the terminology for the different areas of the DOS Shell so you can follow the instructions in the activities. The names and descriptions of the parts of the DOS Shell are:

Title Bar	Displays IBM DOS Shell or MS-DOS Shell.
Menu Bar	Displays names of available drop-down menus from which commands are selected.
Current directory path	Displays the drive and directory path of the directory highlighted in the Directory Tree.

Figure 7-1
DOS Shell

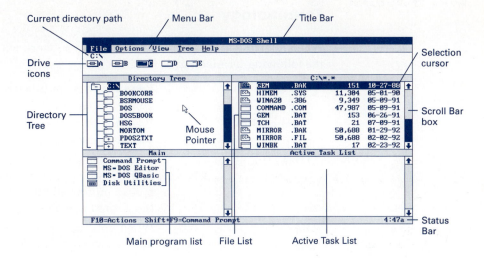

Drive icons	Shows the disk drives available on your computer system. (Notice the difference in appearance of the floppy disk drives [drives A and B] and the hard disk drives [drives C, D, and E].) The current drive is highlighted.
Area titles:	
Directory Tree	Shows directories available on the disk on the current drive.
File List	Shows the files available in the current directory on the current drive.
Main	Shows the program list.
Active Task List	Lists programs available when Task Swapper is activated.
Selection cursor	Highlights the item(s) selected.
Scroll Bars	Shows the listing is too long to fit in the area.
Status Bar	Displays messages from the DOS Shell, shortcut keys, and the current time.
Mouse pointer	Appears only if you have a mouse installed.

NOTE: *Depending upon how DOS 6.0 was installed on your computer, the mouse pointer may be shaped as an arrow, as a rectangular box, or as a square box. When selecting an item, position the point of the arrow or the box on the desired item. The item selected is highlighted and appears on the screen in a different shade or color.*

The DOS Shell acts as a window to let you see information about several areas at one time. The information in the area windows changes as you make selections in the DOS Shell.

Terminology

When referring to an action to be taken as you work with the DOS 6.0 Shell, the following terminology is used:

Click	Press the active button (usually the left button) on the mouse once.
Double-click	Press the active mouse button twice in rapid succession without moving the mouse.
Drag	After positioning the mouse pointer on the desired object, press and hold down the active mouse button while moving the mouse until the desired new position is reached.
Key + Key	When you see a plus sign between two keys, hold down the first key while pressing the second key and then let go of both keys.
Function key	When you see an F followed by a number, press the specified function key.

The activities in this lesson are designed to acquaint you with maneuvering in the DOS Shell and to familiarize you with its different parts. You can work through the activities with or without a mouse. If you have a mouse, you might want to go through the activities twice—once using the keyboard and again using the mouse.

To boot your computer:

1. Boot your computer from the hard drive to the DOS prompt. If necessary, enter the usual startup commands for the path and prompt. Load DOSKEY.

2. Insert your ACTIVITY disk in drive A.

To access the DOS Shell:

1. Type **dosshell** and press [Enter]. Your screen should be similar to Figure 7-1 though the names in the Directory Tree and File List areas are different. As changes in the DOS Shell appearance are saved when the DOS Shell is exited, the appearance of your screen might differ from that in Figure 7-1.

2. If you do not have an area heading under Directory Tree, press [Alt]+[V]. Use [↓] to highlight Program/File Lists and then press [Enter]

3. If the area under the Directory Tree is titled Disk Utilities instead of Main, press [Tab] until Disk Utilities is highlighted. If necessary, press [↓] to highlight Main in the Disk Utilities area. With Main highlighted, press [Enter]

4. If you do not have an area titled Active Task List, press [Alt]+[O]. Use [↓] to highlight Enable Task Swapper and then press [Enter]

EXPLORE THE DOS SHELL

To select areas:

1. Select the Main area heading. (Click the left mouse button with the pointer positioned on it or press [Tab] until Main is highlighted.)

2. Select the Directory Tree heading. (Click the left mouse button with the pointer positioned on it or press [Tab] until Directory Tree is highlighted.)

3. Select the File List area.

4. Select the disk drive area. The letter C beside the hard-drive icon is highlighted.

Look at the drive icons (icons are graphic symbols) on your screen. Notice the difference between the icons for the floppy drive(s) and the hard drive(s).

To select disk drives:

1. Press [←] until A beside the A floppy-drive icon is highlighted. Press [Enter]. Drive A is the current drive and the contents in the Directory Tree and File List area are changed.

2. Change the current drive to drive C by clicking on the drive C icon or by pressing [→] until C is highlighted and then pressing [Enter]

The DOS 6.0 Shell shortcut to change the current drive is to press [Ctrl] plus the letter of the drive you want to make current.

1. Use the shortcut to change the current drive to drive A ([Ctrl]+[A]).

2. Use the shortcut to change the current drive to drive C.

To use the Directory Tree:

1. Select the Directory Tree.

2. If only C:\ is listed, press the plus symbol (+) on the keyboard.

3. Select the second name listed in the Directory Tree by clicking on it (click on the directory name, not on the icon in front of the directory name) or by pressing [↓] to highlight it. The contents of the File List area are now the files in the directory selected in the Directory Tree.

4. Select C:\ in the Directory Tree. (Click on it or press [↑] to highlight it.)

To use the File List:

1. Select the File List area.

2. Select the third file listed in the File List area. (Click on it or press [↓] to highlight it.)

To use the Main area:

1. Select the Main area.

2. Press ⬇ to highlight Disk Utilities or click on Disk Utilities. To execute any command listed in the Main area, you must either double-click on the command or highlight the command (using the arrow keys) and then press Enter

3. Double-click on Disk Utilities or press Enter. Several commands are listed and the area heading is changed to Disk Utilities.

Commands listed under Disk Utilities are executed in the same manner as commands listed under Main. You must either double-click on the command or highlight the command (using the arrow keys) and then press Enter

4. Execute the Main command in the Disk Utilities. Disk Utilities is closed and you are returned to the Main area. Disk Utilities remains highlighted.

Scroll Bars indicate there is more to be viewed than can be displayed in the area window. You can scroll through the area to see the other information.

To use the Scroll Bars:

1. Highlight the Directory Tree heading.

2. Select the DOS directory. The File List heading changes to C:\DOS*.*. The Scroll Bar of the File List area is in two colors or shades to indicate that there are more files to be viewed.

3. Select the File List area. The File List area lists the names of files in the DOS directory on drive C (the current drive).

4. Press Page Down twice. The file listing advances each time Page Down is pressed.

5. Press Page Up twice. The file listing backs up so the initial files are listed.

6. Press End. The names of the last files in the DOS directory on drive C are listed.

7. Press Home. The first files in the DOS directory on drive C are listed.

If you have a mouse:

8. Click three times on ⬇ in the Scroll Bar of the File List area. The listing advances one file each time you click on ⬇

9. Click on the File List Scroll Bar above ⬇. This works the same as using Page Down

10. Click on the File List Scroll Bar under ⬆. This works the same as using Page Up

11. Position the mouse on the box in the File List Scroll Bar. Click and hold down the active mouse button as you drag the box to the bottom of the Scroll Bar. You are now at the end of the file listing.

12. Drag the box in the File List Scroll Bar to the top of the Scroll Bar. You are now at the top of the file listing.

EXIT THE DOS SHELL

The DOS 6.0 Shell gives you several ways to exit. You can exit the Shell temporarily or permanently.

To temporarily exit the DOS Shell:

1. Press [Shift]+[F9]. You have temporarily exited the DOS Shell to the DOS prompt. Unfortunately, the screen does not tell you what to type to return to the DOS Shell.

2. Type **exit** and press [Enter]. You are returned to the DOS Shell.

3. Execute Command Prompt in the Main area. (Double-click on Command Prompt or press [Tab] to highlight Main, press [↓] until Command Prompt is highlighted, and press [Enter].) You have again temporarily exited the DOS Shell.

4. Type **exit** and press [Enter]. You are returned to the DOS Shell.

To permanently exit the DOS Shell:

1. Press [Alt] + [F] and then type **x**. You have permanently exited the DOS Shell.

2. Access the DOS Shell again (**dosshell**).

3. Press [F3]. This is the quickest way to permanently exit the DOS Shell.

4. Access the DOS Shell again (**dosshell**).

MENUS, DIALOG BOXES, AND HELP

Drop-Down Menus

All of the items in the Menu Bar have a drop-down menu. Figure 7-2 shows all the commands available from the Menu Bar items when the Directory Tree or File List areas are highlighted. The shortcuts to execute a command, such

Figure 7-2
Drop-down menu commands

```
         COMMANDS AVAILABLE FROM SHELL DROP-DOWN MENUS
       File                  Options                    View
  Open...                Confirmation...          Single File List
  Run...                 File Display Options...  Dual File Lists
  Print                  Select Across Directories All Files
  Associate...           Show Information...      Program/File Lists
  Search...             *Enable Task Swapper      Program List
  View File Contents F9  Display...               Repaint Screen Shift+F5
  Move...            F7  Colors...                Refresh          F5
  Copy...            F8
  Delete...         Del          Tree                    Help
  Rename...
  Change Atributes...    Expand One Level  +      Keyboard
  Create Directory...    Expand Branch     *      Shell Basics
  Select All             Expand All        Ctrl+* Commands
  Deselect All           Collapse Branch   -      Procedures
  Exit           Alt+F4                           Using Help
                                                  About Shell
```

as Alt+F4 for Exit, are also shown in Figure 7-2. To access a drop-down menu, click on the item name in the Menu Bar or press Alt while typing the first letter of the Menu Bar item.

To access drop-down menus:

1. Change the current drive to drive A using the shortcut (Ctrl+A).

2. Select Directory Tree.

3. Select Options in the Menu Bar (click on it or press Alt+O).

4. Close the drop-down menu by pressing the right mouse button or Esc.

5. Select View in the Menu Bar (click on it or press Alt+V).

6. Press → or click on Tree in the Menu Bar to close the View drop-down menu and open the Tree drop-down menu.

7. Close the Tree drop-down menu.

Dimmed Commands

When looking at the drop-down menus, some commands appear in much lighter print. These are called **dimmed commands**. A dimmed command is unavailable for execution. If a file has not been selected, for instance, commands such as Copy, Move, or Rename in the File drop-down menu are dimmed and not available for execution.

To explore dimmed commands:

1. Select File in the Menu Bar.

    Several of the commands are dimmed. They are not available for execution as no file has been selected.

2. Close the File drop-down menu.

3. Select the File List area. The first file in the area is automatically highlighted.

4. Select File in the Menu Bar. With a file selected, only one command is dimmed and unavailable for execution.

5. Close the File drop-down menu.

6. Select the Main area.

7. Select File in the Menu Bar. With a command in the Main area highlighted, the commands available in the File drop-down menu are changed and Tree is no longer available in the Menu Bar.

8. Close the File drop-down menu.

Dialog Boxes

To execute a command from a drop-down menu, position the mouse pointer on it and click the active mouse button. Without a mouse, type the underlined letter of the desired command. You can also select a command by pressing ↓ or ↑ until the desired command is highlighted and then press Enter to execute the command.

Some of the commands shown in Figure 7-2 are followed by three periods (...), called **ellipses**. The ellipses indicate that when the command is selected DOS will need more information to execute it. DOS 6.0 uses a **dialog box** to request information it needs to execute a command. Figure 7-3 shows the dialog box when Rename is selected from the File drop-down menu. The file previously selected is displayed, and DOS needs to know the new filename in order to execute the command. The oval-shaped buttons near the bottom of the dialog box are **command buttons**. A dialog box command is executed by clicking on the desired button.

Figure 7-3
Sample dialog box

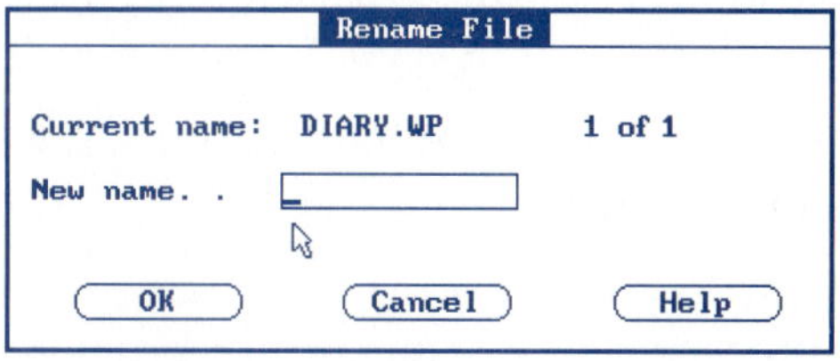

To explore dialog boxes:

1. Drive A should be the current drive. If not, change the current drive to drive A (Ctrl+A).

2. Select the File List area.

3. Access the File drop-down menu.
4. Execute the Re<u>n</u>ame command in the drop-down menu.

   The name of the file highlighted in the File List area is shown. The cursor is set for you to enter the first character of the new filename.

5. Cancel the dialog box by clicking on the Cancel button at the bottom of the dialog box or pressing [Esc]. When a dialog box is canceled, you are returned to the DOS Shell.

6. Select File in the Menu Bar.

7. Execute the <u>C</u>opy command.

   The name of the file highlighted in the File List area is displayed in the From: information box. The cursor is positioned behind the A:\ in the To: information box waiting for you to type where you want the file to be copied.

8. Cancel the dialog box using the same procedure as you did in step 5 of this activity.

HELP

When in the DOS Shell, you can access HELP from the Menu Bar or press [F1] as a shortcut. The information displayed in the HELP dialog box depends upon the command or area of the shell highlighted prior to pressing [F1].

To explore HELP in the DOS Shell:

1. Select HELP in the Menu Bar.

2. Execute <u>S</u>hell Basics in the drop-down menu.

3. After reading the dialog box, press [Page Down]. "Welcome to DOS Shell" is highlighted.

4. Execute the topic "Dialog Box" (double-click on it or press [Tab] until it is highlighted and then press [Enter]).

5. Return to the previous screen by clicking on the Back command button or by pressing [Tab] until the cursor is positioned in the Back button and then press [Enter]

6. Select "Welcome to DOS Shell" (click on it or press [Shift]+[Tab] to move the cursor backwards until it is highlighted).

7. Close the dialog box (click on Close or press [Esc]).

8. Highlight the Directory Tree area.

9. Press F1. The HELP dialog box on "File List Overview" is displayed.
10. Close the HELP dialog box.

DOS SHELL DIRECTORY TREE

The DOS 6.0 Directory Tree is similar to the directory structure displayed with the TREE command (see Lesson Four). The plus (+) and minus (–) symbols in some of the file-folder icons in Figure 7-4 indicate whether or not the subdirectory names are displayed.

Figure 7-4
A partial Directory Tree

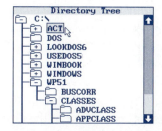

To explore the Directory Tree:

1. Change the current drive to drive C (Ctrl+C).
2. Select the ROOT directory in the Directory Tree.
3. Execute Collapse Branch from the Tree drop-down menu. All the subdirectories of the ROOT directory are hidden.
4. Execute Expand One Level from the Tree drop-down menu. Only the subdirectories of the ROOT directory are displayed. Some of the icons in front of the directory names may be filled with a plus sign (+) to indicate that they have subdirectories.
5. Highlight the ACT directory.
6. Execute Expand Branch from the Tree drop-down menu. All the subdirectories (TRAVEL, WORDPRO, and WORDPRO\BUSINESS) are displayed. Other subdirectories of ROOT are not expanded.
7. Execute Expand All from the Tree drop-down menu. The entire directory structure of the hard drive is displayed.
8. Select the ROOT directory.

To change the size of the Directory Tree and File List areas:

1. Execute Single File List from the View drop-down menu to lengthen the Directory Tree and File List areas. The Main and Active Task List areas are no longer shown.

2. Select Tree in the Menu Bar. Notice that all the commands have a shortcut listed to the right. Go through the steps in the last activity again, using the shortcuts to execute the commands. With a mouse, you can click on the icon in front of a directory name containing a + or – symbol instead of pressing the + or – on the keyboard.

3. Highlight the ROOT directory. Do whatever is necessary so that just the subdirectories of the ROOT directory are displayed.

4. Execute Program/File Lists from the View drop-down menu to reduce the Directory Tree and File List areas so that the screen also shows the commands in the Main and Active Task List areas.

THE FILE LIST AREA

The File List area lists files in the directory highlighted in the Directory Tree. Using the File Display Options command in the Options drop-down menu, you can specify the order in which you wish to view the file listing. The default file order when DOS 6.0 is installed is alphabetically by filename. Figure 7-5 shows the dialog box for the File Display Options command.

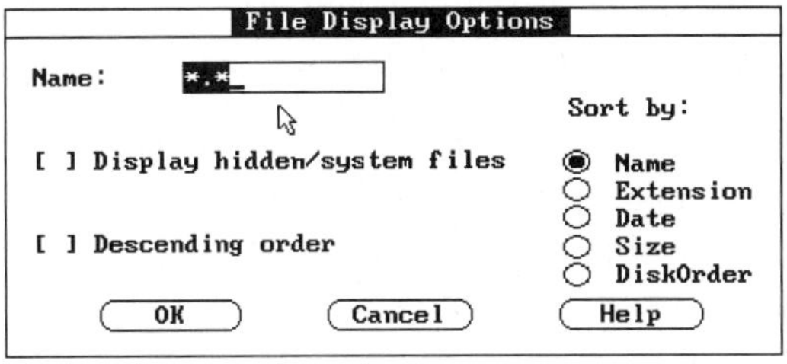

Figure 7-5
File Display Options dialog box

NOTE: *When working with the Name: box, pressing* [Spacebar], [Backspace], *or typing without first pressing* [←] *or* [→] *erases everything in the box.*

To change the order of files listed:

1. Change the current drive to drive A. Highlight the File List area.

2. Execute File Display Options in the Options drop-down menu. The cursor is behind the *.* in the Name: box.

3. Select Descending order. (Click on it or press [Tab] until the cursor is in the brackets in front of it and press [Spacebar].) An X fills the brackets to show that it is selected. Both items with brackets are toggle switches and are turned on and off by clicking within the brackets or by pressing [Spacebar] with the cursor positioned within the brackets.

4. Click on OK or press [Enter] to execute the File Display Options dialog box command. The files in the File List are in reverse order by name.

To sort the files listed:

1. Execute File Display Options in the Options drop-down menu.

2. Toggle off the Descending order choice.

3. Select Extension in the Sort by: column. (Click on it or press [Tab] to move to the Sort by: column and then press [↓].) Execute the dialog box command.

NOTE: *When pressing [Tab], you cannot see the cursor anywhere in the dialog box when it is in the Sort by: column.*

4. Execute File Display Options from the Options drop-down menu and select Size in the Sort by: column. Execute the dialog box command.

To selectively list files:

1. Execute File Display Options from the Options drop-down menu.

2. The cursor is behind the *.* in the Name: box. Press [←]. The cursor moves in the Name: box to under the first character. Type **p** so the command reads p*.* and then execute the dialog box command.

The files starting with the letter P are listed by size.

3. Execute File Display Options from the Options drop-down menu. Change the Name: box so it reads x*.* and execute the dialog box command.

4. Execute File Display Options from the Options drop-down menu. Type ***.com**. As soon as you begin to type, the previous contents in the Name: box are erased. Execute the dialog box command.

5. Execute File Display Options. Type *.* in the Name: box. Select Name in the Sort by: column. Execute the command.

6. Change the current drive to drive C.

A major plus of the DOS Shell is the ability to display a directory listing of two directories on the same screen. Figure 7-6 shows the Directory Tree and File List areas of both drive C and drive A.

Figure 7-6
Dual File List screen

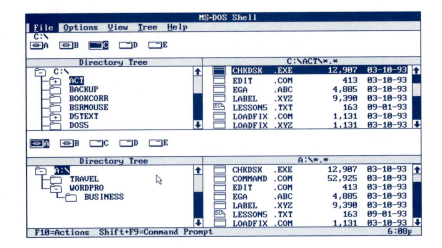

To use the dual file listing:

1. Execute Dual File Lists from View. Your screen now is split horizontally with the Directory Tree and File List of drive C on both the top and bottom of the screen.

2. Change the current drive to drive A in the lower portion of the DOS Shell. (Click on it or press [Tab] until drive C is highlighted in the lower portion of your screen and then press [Ctrl]+[A].)

3. Select Program/File Lists from View. The DOS Shell is changed to show only the current drive with the File List area reduced.

To turn off the computer:

1. Execute Exit from the File drop-down menu to permanently exit the DOS Shell.

2. Turn off the computer and monitor.

3. Remove your ACTIVITY disk from drive A.

■ SUMMARY OF COMMANDS

Topic or Feature	Command or Key	Shortcut	Page
Access DOS Shell	DOSSHELL		70
Select DOS Shell area	Click on area heading, [Tab], or [Shift]+[Tab]		71
Change current drive	[Tab] and arrow keys or click on drive icon	[Ctrl]+drive letter	71

Topic or Feature	Command or Key	Shortcut	Page
View Disk Utilities commands	Main |Disk Utilities	Double-click	72
Scroll through listing	Page Up, Page Down, Home, End, and arrow keys	Click in Scroll Bar	72
Temporarily exit Shell	Main |Command Prompt	Shift+F9	73
Return to Shell after temporary exit	EXIT		73
Permanently exit Shell	File |Exit	Alt+F4 or F3	73
Access Menu Bar item	Tab and arrow keys or click on Menu Bar item	Alt+first letter of Menu Bar item	74
Close drop-down menu	Esc or click right mouse button		74
Execute drop-down menu command	Highlight and press Enter or click on command	Type underlined letter of command	75
Access Help	Alt+H	F1	76
Display subdirectories of current directory	Tree |Expand One Level	+	77
Collapse subdirectories of current directory	Tree |Collapse Branch	−	77
Display all subdirectories of current directory	Tree |Expand Branch	*	77
Display entire directory structure	Tree |Expand All	Ctrl+*	77
Expand Directory Tree and File List areas	View |Single File List		78
Reduce Directory Tree and File List areas	View |Program/File Lists		78
Selectively view files	Options |File Display Options		78
Display two Directory Trees and File Lists	View |Dual File Lists		80

■ REVIEW QUESTIONS

1. To access the DOS Shell from the DOS prompt, type _____.
2. The directories of a disk are listed in the _____ area of the DOS Shell.
3. When a directory name is highlighted, the listing in the File List area (changes/does not change) _____ to show the files in the selected directory.
4. To select File in the Menu Bar, _____ on File or press _____.
5. When a command in a drop-down menu is dimmed, it (is/is not) _____ available for execution.
6. Commands in a drop-down menu followed by ellipses (...) use a _____ to request more information.
7. The DOS Shell (does/does not) _____ allow you to view files on two disks at the same time.
8. To permanently exit the DOS Shell, execute _____ in the File drop-down menu or press _____.
9. After temporarily exiting the DOS Shell, type _____ to return to the Shell.
10. Pressing the _____ key is a shortcut to expand the highlighted directory one level.

■ HANDS-ON EXERCISES

Exercise 7-1 Boot your computer to the DOS prompt from the hard drive. If necessary, enter the usual startup commands for the path and prompt. Load DOSKEY. Insert your ACTIVITY disk into drive A. Access the DOS Shell. Practice using the shortcuts and the Tree drop-down menu to collapse and expand the Directory Tree listing. Change the current drive to drive A. Temporarily exit the DOS Shell. Return to the DOS Shell and change the current drive to drive C.

Exercise 7-2 Select the DOS directory in the Directory Tree on drive C. Select the File List area. Use File Display Options in the Options drop-down menu to selectively list the following:

1. Files with an EXE extension sorted by size
2. Files starting with the letter D in reverse (descending) order sorted by extension

3. All files in normal order sorted by name

Change the DOS Shell so it displays the Directory Tree and File List areas of both drive A and drive C. Change the DOS Shell so it displays only drive A. Permanently exit the DOS Shell. Turn off the computer and monitor. Remove your disk.

LESSON EIGHT DOS Shell Commands

OBJECTIVES

In this lesson you will learn how to:

- Format a disk from the DOS Shell.
- Make, remove, and rename directories from the DOS Shell.
- Copy and move files.
- Delete and undelete files.
- Execute DOS prompt commands without leaving the DOS Shell.

Now that you have learned to use several DOS commands from the DOS prompt, this lesson shows you how to execute the same commands from the DOS Shell. Executing commands from the DOS Shell will provide you with a review of previously learned commands. Also, DOS has a few commands that can only be executed from the DOS Shell; they are not available from the DOS prompt.

FORMAT

FORMAT is one of the commands listed under Disk Utilities in the Main area. When FORMAT is selected, a dialog box appears. The dialog box shows **a:** in the Parameters information box. Like the Name: box in the File Display Options dialog box, if you press [Spacebar], [Backspace], or start typing without first pressing an arrow key, the information in the Parameters box is erased. To add a switch to the FORMAT command, first press [→] and then type the desired switch(es).

When commands in the Disk Utilities are executed, the DOS Shell is temporarily exited. The command is executed just as it is from the DOS prompt. After the command execution, the message "Press any key to return to the DOS Shell" appears in the lower right corner of the screen.

To boot your computer:

1. Boot your computer from the hard drive to the DOS prompt. Enter a temporary path to the DOS and ROOT directories on drive C (**path=c:\dos;c:**). If necessary, change the DOS prompt. Load DOSKEY.

2. Access the DOS Shell.

To format a nonsystem disk:

1. Insert your NUMONE disk into drive A.
2. Execute Disk Utilities in the Main area.
3. Execute Format from the list of Disk Utilities commands.
4. The cursor is positioned behind **a:** in the Parameters box in the Format dialog box. Click on OK or press [Enter]
5. A screen message prompts you to insert a disk in drive A. With your NUMONE disk in drive A, press [Enter] to proceed with the formatting.
6. Type your first name when prompted to enter the Volume label.
7. Type **n** and press [Enter] when asked whether you want to format another disk. Press any key to return to the DOS Shell.

To format a system disk:

1. Execute Format from the Disk Utilities.
2. Press [→] once. The highlighting of **a:** is removed. Type the switch used to create a system disk (**/s**).
3. Proceed with the formatting. When requested, type your last name as the Volume label. Type **n** and press [Enter] when asked whether you want to format another disk. Press any key to return to the DOS Shell.
4. Change the current drive to drive A.
5. Execute Main in the Disk Utilities so that the Main commands are displayed.

DIRECTORIES

Make a Directory

To make a directory in the DOS Shell takes two steps: highlight the name of the directory you wish to divide and execute the Create Directory command from the File drop-down menu. The dialog box shown in Figure 8-1 appears on the screen. The cursor is positioned in the New Directory Name box. After you have typed the new directory name, choose OK or press [Enter] to create the directory.

To make a directory:

1. Your NUMONE disk is in drive A and drive A is the current drive.

Figure 8-1
Create Directory dialog box

2. Select the Directory Tree area. The ROOT directory is automatically highlighted.

3. Execute the Create Directory command from the File drop-down menu.

4. Type **music** and press [Enter] to create a directory named MUSIC.

5. Select MUSIC as the current directory.

6. Execute the Create Directory command. In the New Directory Name box of the dialog box, type ***xxx** and press [Enter]

Look at the error message. From the DOS Shell you can only create a subdirectory to the current directory. By entering \XXX, you instructed DOS to make the directory XXX as a subdirectory of ROOT.

7. Cancel the command (click on Cancel or press [Esc]).

To make a directory:

1. Select the ROOT directory.

2. Create SSFILE as a subdirectory of the ROOT directory.

3. Create WPFILE as a subdirectory of the ROOT directory.

4. Select WPFILE in the Directory Tree.

5. Create NOTES as a subdirectory of WPFILE.

6. Create HOMEWORK as a subdirectory of WPFILE.

7. Select HOMEWORK in the Directory Tree.

8. Create PAPERS as a subdirectory of HOMEWORK.

Rename a Directory

Though directories cannot be renamed from the DOS prompt, you can rename directories through the DOS Shell.

To rename a directory:

1. Select MUSIC in the Directory Tree.

2. Execute Rename in the File drop-down menu.

3. Type **sports** and press [Enter]. The new directory name is seen immediately in the Directory Tree.

4. Rename the directory PAPERS to REPORTS.

To set up your system to confirm your actions, Confirmation is selected from the Options drop-down menu. With Confirm on Delete toggled on, DOS checks whenever you delete a file or directory. The Confirmation dialog box, shown in Figure 8-2, shows all of the confirmation choices toggled on.

Figure 8-2
The Confirmation dialog box

To set confirmation:

1. Execute Confirmation from the Options drop-down menu.

2. If the brackets in front of Confirm on Delete do not contain an X, toggle on Confirm on Delete. Click in the bracket in front of the item to toggle the choice on or press [Tab] until the cursor is positioned in the bracket and press [Spacebar] to toggle the choice on.

3. If the other choices listed in the dialog box do not contain an X, toggle on all the choices.

4. Choose OK to execute the choices you made in the Confirmation dialog box.

Remove a Directory

Unlike removing a directory from the DOS prompt, in the DOS Shell the directory to be removed must be the current directory. From looking at the File List area, you can tell whether the directory you want to remove contains any files that must be copied, erased, or moved before removing the directory.

To remove a directory:

1. If all of the directories are not visible, press [Ctrl]+[*] to expand the entire Directory Tree.

2. Select the HOMEWORK directory.

3. Execute Delete from the File drop-down menu. As HOMEWORK has a subdirectory, it is not empty. The Deletion Error dialog box explains why HOMEWORK cannot be deleted.

4. Close the Deletion Error dialog box.
5. Select the NOTES directory.
6. Execute the Delete command from the File drop-down menu.
7. The cursor is in the Yes button in the Delete Directory Confirmation dialog box. Click on Yes or press [Enter]
8. Select the REPORTS directory. Press [Del]. Respond Yes in the Delete Directory Confirmation dialog box.
9. Remove the SPORTS directory using [Del]

COPY AND MOVE FILES

Copy

Files can be copied using the Copy command or by dragging the files with a mouse. Using either Copy or its shortcut, [F8], brings up a dialog box in which you enter the destination. As shown in Figure 8-3, the highlighted filename is already entered in the From: box in the Copy File dialog box and the current drive and directory are entered in the To: box.

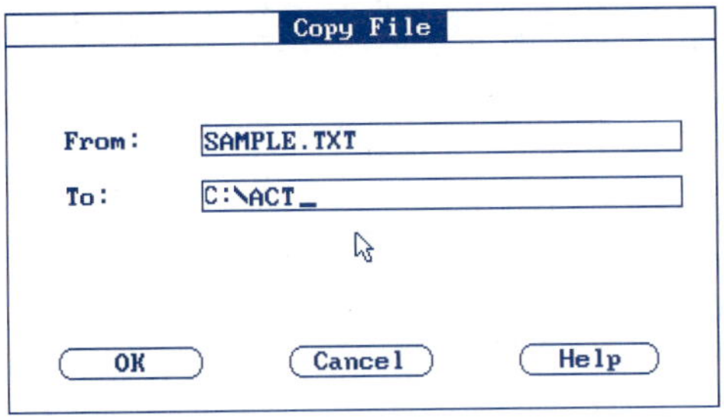

Figure 8-3
The Copy File dialog box

To copy files:

1. Execute Dual File Lists from the View drop-down menu. The Directory Tree for drive A is visible in the upper half of the screen and the Directory Tree for drive C is visible in the lower half.
2. Select the ACT directory on drive C in the lower half of the screen.
3. If necessary, expand the ACT directory so all the subdirectories are visible (press *).
4. Highlight the file EDIT.COM in the ACT directory.
5. Execute Copy in the File drop-down menu.

Lesson 8/DOS Shell Commands

6. The cursor is positioned behind C:\ACT in the To: box. Type **a:** and press [Enter]. The contents of the To: box are erased as soon as you begin typing. The file is copied to the ROOT directory on drive A.

7. Highlight the file MORE.COM in the ACT directory.

8. Press [F8]. The Copy dialog box immediately appears on the screen.

9. Type **a:** and press [Enter]. The file is copied to drive A, ROOT directory.

With a mouse, you can drag a file to the destination directory. As Confirm on Mouse Operation was one of the Confirmation choices you toggled on earlier, a dialog box will appear to have you confirm the operation whenever you use the mouse to drag a file. To copy a file to another drive, press and hold down the active button while you drag the file onto the destination directory on the Directory Tree.

To copy a file by dragging:

(If you do not have a mouse, copy the files to the ROOT directory on drive A using the Copy command.)

1. Highlight the file EGA.ABC in the ACT directory.

2. Press and hold down the active mouse button while you drag the file onto A:\ in the Directory Tree of drive A. As the file is dragged over the Directory Tree, the directories are highlighted. When A:\ is highlighted, release the active button. The file is copied.

3. Click on Yes in the Mouse Confirmation box.

4. Highlight the file TAG.EXE in the ACT directory. Drag the file onto A:\ in the Directory Tree of drive A.

The procedure to copy files to another directory on the same drive by dragging is slightly different than dragging the files to another drive. After highlighting the file to be copied, hold down [Ctrl] while pressing the active mouse button and dragging the file onto the destination directory in the Directory Tree on the same drive.

> **CAUTION: First highlight the file and then hold down [Ctrl] to drag the file to a directory on the same drive. If you hold down [Ctrl] while highlighting the file to be copied, the file highlighted before pressing [Ctrl] will also be copied.**

To copy files to another directory on the same drive:

1. Execute Single File List in the View drop-down menu.

2. If necessary, change the current drive to drive A.

3. If necessary, press [Ctrl]+[*] to expand the entire Directory Tree.

4. Select A:\ in the Directory Tree. All the files previously copied are listed.

5. Select the file EGA.ABC.

6. Without a mouse:

    a. Execute Copy from the File drop-down menu.

    b. As a:\ is already entered in the To: box, press [→] first, type **wpfile** and press [Enter]. The To: box should read a:\wpfile.

7. With a mouse, hold down [Ctrl] while you drag the file onto WPFILE in the Directory Tree.

8. As the Confirmation is on, click on Yes or press [Enter] in the Confirmation dialog box.

9. Highlight the file EDIT.COM in the A:\ File List area. Follow the procedure of step 6 or step 7 to copy the file to the WPFILE directory.

10. Select WPFILE in the Directory Tree. The two files you just copied are listed.

11. Select A:\ in the Directory Tree. The two files you just copied are still listed.

Move

Files can be moved using the Move command in the File drop-down menu or by dragging the files with a mouse. Using either Move or its shortcut, [F7], brings up a dialog box in which you enter the destination.

To move a file:

1. Select the file EDIT.COM in the A:\ directory.

2. Without a mouse:

    a. Press [F7]. The Move dialog box appears on the screen.

    b. Press [→] before typing **ssfile** and pressing [Enter] to move the file from the ROOT directory to the SSFILE directory on drive A.

3. With a mouse, hold down [Alt] while you drag the file onto the SSFILE directory in the Directory Tree.

4. As the Confirmation is on, click on Yes or press [Enter] in the Confirmation dialog box.

5. Highlight the file EGA.ABC in the A:\ directory. Follow the same procedure as step 2 or step 3 to move the file to the SSFILE directory on drive A.

DELETE AND UNDELETE FILES

Delete

To delete a file, first highlight the file and then execute Delete from the File drop-down menu or press [Del]

To delete files:

1. Execute Program/File Lists in the View drop-down menu.
2. If necessary, press [Ctrl]+[*] to expand the entire Directory Tree.
3. Highlight the ROOT directory on drive A.
4. Highlight TAG.EXE in the file list area.
5. Execute Delete in the File drop-down menu to delete TAG.EXE.
6. When the dialog box appears, confirm the deletion.
7. Highlight MORE.COM in the ROOT directory. Press [Del]. When the dialog box appears, confirm the deletion.

Undelete

If you delete a file by mistake, you can undelete it from the DOS Shell by executing the Undelete command available in the Disk Utilities in the Main area. Figure 8-4 shows the dialog box when Undelete is executed.

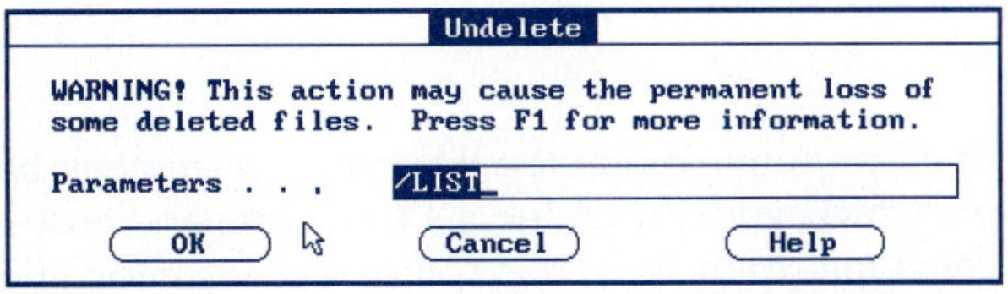

Figure 8-4
Undelete dialog box

Like the Format command, the DOS Shell is temporarily exited while the command is executed. After returning to the DOS Shell, do not be alarmed when the recovered file is not shown in the File List area. Instead, highlight the File List heading and then execute Refresh from the View drop-down menu (or press [F5] as a shortcut).

To undelete files:

1. Execute Disk Utilities in the Main area.

2. Execute Undelete. The Undelete dialog box initially shows a /LIST switch that lists the files deleted in the current directory.

3. Type **tag.exe** in the Parameters box and execute the dialog box command.

4. After returning to the DOS Shell, the undeleted file is not listed.

5. Highlight the File List heading. Press [F5] to refresh the screen.

6. Highlight the ROOT directory. Execute Undelete to undelete the file MORE.COM. After returning to the DOS Shell, refresh the screen.

7. Execute Main in the Disk Utilities to close the Disk Utilities commands.

Change Disks

If you switch floppy disks in a drive, DOS must be prompted to know you have switched disks.

To change disks:

1. Remove your NUMONE disk and insert your ACTIVITY disk into drive A. DOS doesn't know that you have switched disks. The Directory Tree is still that of your NUMONE disk.

2. Highlight the File List area heading and then press [F5] to refresh the screen. In a few moments the Directory Tree and File List of your ACTIVITY disk are displayed.

RUN

The Run command in the File drop-down menu brings up a command line on which you can enter a DOS command just as you would enter the command from the DOS prompt. For instance, after bringing up the dialog box and typing TREE /F > PRN, the directory structure and files in each directory of the current drive are printed. If the current directory is not ROOT, you can print the directory structure and files starting with the ROOT directory by entering TREE \ /F > PRN.

To use the Run command:

1. Turn on the printer and properly position the paper.

2. Highlight the ROOT directory of drive A in the Directory Tree.

3. Execute Run in the File drop-down menu.

4. Type **tree /f > prn** and press Enter. The directory structure and files in each directory are printed. Press any key to return to the DOS Shell.

5. Execute Run in the File drop-down menu.

6. Type **date** and press Enter. The current system date is displayed and you are prompted to enter the date.

7. Press Enter to accept the displayed date. Press any key to return to the DOS Shell.

8. Advance the paper in the printer and remove your printout.

9. Permanently exit the DOS Shell.

To turn off your computer:

1. Turn off your printer, computer, and monitor.

2. Remove your disk.

■ SUMMARY OF COMMANDS

Topic or Feature	Command or Key	Shortcut	Page
Format a disk	Main ¦ Disk Utilities ¦ Format		85
Make a directory	File ¦ Create Directory		85
Rename a directory	File ¦ Rename		86
Remove a directory	File ¦ Delete	Del	87
Change confirmation choices	Options ¦ Confirmation		87
Copy a file to another drive	File ¦ Copy or drag file	F8	88
Copy a file to another directory on the same drive	File ¦ Copy or Ctrl + drag file	F8	89
Move a file	File ¦ Move or Alt + drag file	F7	90
Delete a file	File ¦ Delete	Del	91
Undelete a file	Main ¦ Disk Utilities ¦ Undelete		92
Reread a disk's files	View ¦ Refresh	F5	92
Execute a DOS prompt command from the DOS Shell	File ¦ Run		92

■ REVIEW QUESTIONS

1. The Format command in the DOS Shell is one of the commands in the _____.

2. When creating a directory, you (can/cannot) _____ create it as a subdirectory to any directory.

3. To remove an empty directory, highlight the directory name in the Directory Tree and press _____.

4. The shortcut for the <u>C</u>opy command in the File drop-down menu is _____.

5. To copy a file to another directory on the same disk by dragging the file, you (do/do not) _____ hold down Ctrl while dragging the file.

6. The shortcut for the <u>M</u>ove command in the File drop-down menu is _____.

7. To move a file by dragging it, hold down _____ while dragging the file to the destination directory in the Directory Tree.

8. To tell DOS that you have switched disks, press _____ to have DOS reread the file allocation table (FAT) and refresh the screen.

9. To execute DOS prompt commands that are not available in the DOS Shell, use the _____ command.

10. A directory (can/cannot) _____ be renamed from the DOS prompt. A directory (can/cannot) _____ be renamed from the DOS Shell.

■ HANDS-ON EXERCISES

Exercise 8-1

Boot your computer from drive C to the DOS prompt. If necessary, enter the usual startup commands for the path and prompt. Load DOSKEY. Insert your NUMONE disk into drive A. Access the DOS Shell. Format the NUMONE disk in drive A as a system disk with PRAC8 as the volume label. Change the current drive to drive A and create the following directories on your NUMONE disk:

1. TESTDIR as a subdirectory of ROOT
2. PRACTICE as a subdirectory of TESTDIR

Exercise 8-2

Change the Shell appearance so you can see the Directory Tree and File List areas of both drive C and drive A. Copy the following files from the ACT directory on drive C to the indicated directories on drive A:

1. EGA.ABC to the ROOT directory on drive A

2. TAG.EXE to TESTDIR

3. EGA.ABC to PRACTICE

Turn on the printer. Execute the command to print the entire directory structure and files on drive A.

Exercise 8-3

Change the appearance of the Shell so you can see the Main and Active Task List areas. Drive A should be the current drive.

1. Move EGA.ABC from the PRACTICE directory to TESTDIR.

2. Remove the PRACTICE directory.

3. Rename TESTDIR to LESSON8.

4. Exit the DOS Shell.

Print the directory structure and files on drive A. Remove your printout. Turn off the printer, computer, and monitor. Remove your NUMONE disk.

LESSON NINE Edit

OBJECTIVES

In this lesson you will learn how to:

- Load EDIT from the DOS prompt.
- Create a file.
- Revise a file and save it with a new name.
- Open an existing file for editing.
- Select text to copy, move, and delete.
- Copy and move text within a document.
- Delete text.

In Lesson Five you were briefly introduced to EDIT when you created a couple of files on your ACTIVITY disk. When creating a file or editing an existing file, EDIT functions as a limited word-processing program.

To boot your computer:

1. Boot your computer from the hard drive to the DOS prompt. If necessary, enter the usual startup PATH and PROMPT commands. Load DOSKEY.
2. Insert your ACTIVITY disk into drive A and change the current drive to drive A.

CREATE A FILE

When EDIT is loaded into memory from the DOS prompt without the name of a file to edit, a dialog box welcomes you to the DOS Editor program. Figure 9-1 shows the dialog box when EDIT is loaded into memory from the DOS Shell.

To load EDIT:

1. Type **edit** and press [Enter]. A "Welcome to the MS-DOS Editor" dialog box gives you the choice of viewing the EDIT Survival Guide or going directly into EDIT.

Figure 9-1
DOS Shell EDIT dialog box

2. As the Survival Guide is an EDIT HELP screen, press [Esc] to clear the dialog box.

As you did not enter the name of a file, the name Untitled is shown near the top of the screen. The cursor is blinking in the upper left corner. EDIT does not let you set margins as does a word-processing program.

To enter text:

1. Type the following. Press [Enter] at the end of each line.

   ASCII is a common coding scheme used by microcomputers. You can save a database file in ASCII and import it to your favorite word-processing program.

2. Look at the cursor position. The status bar shows line 4, position 1. (If the Status Bar shows you are on line 3, press [Enter] so you are on line 4, position 1.) EDIT does not automatically wrap text at the end of a line as do word-processing programs.

The Menu Bar is accessed the same way you accessed it in the DOS Shell. Commands in a drop-down menu are executed by clicking on the command, highlighting the command and pressing [Enter], or by typing the letter that appears in a different color or shade in the command.

To save your file:

1. Execute File in the Menu Bar (click on it or press [Alt]+[F]).

2. Execute **S**ave.

Below the File Name: box, A:\ is displayed as the current path. The cursor is blinking in the File Name: box.

3. Type **coding.txt** and press [Enter]. The file is saved in the ROOT directory on drive A and you are returned to the EDIT screen. CODING.TXT has replaced Untitled near the top of the screen.

With a mouse, when the cursor is at the desired position, click the active mouse button to set the cursor. Without a mouse, use the arrow keys to move the cursor. Pressing [Home] moves the cursor to the beginning of the current line; [End] moves the cursor to the end of the current line.

EDIT is automatically in Insert mode. In Insert mode, the cursor is a blinking underline character. Pressing [Ins] changes the cursor to a blinking rectangle, showing that EDIT is in Strikeover mode. In Strikeover mode, characters you type replace existing characters at the cursor position.

To edit the text:

1. Position and set the cursor on line 1, position 1. The cursor should be a blinking underline character.

2. Type your first and last names. As you are in Insert mode, your name is inserted at the beginning of line 1, moving the text to the right as you type.

3. The cursor should be under the A of ASCII after your last name on line 1. Press [Enter] twice.

4. Position the cursor under the first letter of your last name.

5. Press [Ins]

6. Type your middle initial. In Strikeover mode, your initial replaces the first character of your last name.

7. Press [Ins]. Press [Spacebar] and type the first letter of your last name. The line should now show your first name, middle initial, and last name.

To save the file with a new name:

1. Execute File in the Menu Bar.

2. Execute Save **As** in the drop-down menu.

3. Press [←] to position the cursor under the period after the G of CODING. Type **1** to change the filename to CODING1.TXT. Press [Enter]

4. You are returned to the EDIT screen. CODING1.TXT is shown near the top of your screen as the current file.

When **S**ave is selected from the File drop-down menu, the edited file replaces the original file on the disk. By using Save **A**s, you can enter a new name for the edited file. This way you have both the original and changed files saved on your disk.

MODIFY A FILE

To clear the screen and open an existing file:

1. Execute File in the Menu Bar.

2. Execute **N**ew. The screen is immediately cleared. If you execute **N**ew without first saving the file on the screen, EDIT will remind you that your file has changed and give you a chance to save it. You do not, however, have a chance to specify a new name.

3. Execute **F**ile in the Menu Bar. Execute **O**pen.

Only files with a TXT extension in the current directory are listed. To change drives or directories, double-click on the desired drive and/or directory or use [Tab] and arrow keys to highlight the desired drive and/or directory and press [Enter].

4. Load CODING1.TXT into memory for editing. (Click on the desired file or press [Tab] until the cursor is positioned in the list of files. Use the arrow keys to move the cursor to CODING1.TXT.)

5. With CODING1.TXT in the Name: box, click on OK or press [Enter]

The EDIT commands Cu**t**, **C**opy, **P**aste, and Cl**e**ar all work with selected text. To select text, hold down the active button of the mouse while dragging the cursor over the desired text to highlight it. From the keyboard, text is selected by holding down [Shift] while moving the cursor. Once text has been selected (highlighted) it can be deleted, copied, or moved. When Cu**t** or **C**opy is executed, the selected text is copied to a buffer called the Clipboard. It can then be **P**asted into a document.

To select and deselect text:

1. Select all the text on line 1. (Drag the mouse over the entire line or hold down [Shift] while pressing [End])

2. Remove the highlighting by pressing [Esc] or by moving the mouse pointer elsewhere in the document and clicking the active button.

NOTE: If you accidentally press the wrong mouse button, the EDIT HELP Survival Guide is displayed. Press [Esc] to return to EDIT.

To copy selected text:

1. Select all the text on line 1.

2. Execute **C**opy from the Edit drop-down menu.

3. Move the cursor and set the position on the blank line below the text on the screen (line 6, position 1).

4. Execute **P**aste from the Edit drop-down menu. The line with your name is copied into your document at the cursor position.

To move selected text:

1. Select all the text on line 3.

2. Execute Cu**t** from the Edit drop-down menu. The text on line 3 is immediately removed from your document.

3. Position and set the cursor on the blank line below your name at the end of your document.

4. Execute **P**aste from the Edit drop-down menu. Line 3 is immediately pasted into your document at the cursor position.

To delete selected text:

1. Select the word common in the line you just pasted to the end of your document.

2. Execute **Clear** from the Edit drop-down menu. The word common is removed from the line.

3. Select the word favorite on line 4 of your document. Press [Del]. The selected word is removed from your document.

To print part or all of your document:

1. Select all the text on lines 4, 5, and 6 of your document.

2. Execute **Print** from the File drop-down menu. As some of the document's lines were selected before executing **Print**, an asterisk fills the bracket in front of Selected Text Only.

3. Turn on the printer.

4. Press [Enter]. Only the selected lines of your document are printed.

5. Execute **Print** from the File drop-down menu.

6. Press [↓] to move the asterisk to the brackets in front of Complete Document.

7. Press [Enter]. Your entire document is printed.

To exit EDIT:

1. Execute **Exit** from the File drop-down menu. As your file has changed, EDIT checks whether you want to save the loaded document.

2. Click on No or [Tab] to No and press [Enter]. You are returned to the DOS prompt.

To turn off your computer:

1. Remove your printout. Turn off the printer.

2. Turn off your computer and monitor. Remove your disk.

■ SUMMARY OF COMMANDS

Topic or Feature	Command or Key Shortcut	Page
Load EDIT	EDIT	96
Toggle between Insert and Strikeover modes	[Ins]	97
Save a file	File ¦ **Save**	97
Save a file with a new name	File ¦ **Save As**	98

Topic or Feature	Command or Key	Shortcut	Page
Clear the screen	File ¦ New		98
Open an existing file	File ¦ Open		99
Copy selected text into Clipboard	Edit ¦ Copy	Ctrl+Ins	99
Move selected text into Clipboard	Edit ¦ Cut	Shift+Del	99
Copy selected text from Clipboard	Edit ¦ Paste	Shift+Ins	99
Delete selected text	Edit ¦ Clear	Del	100
Print selected text	File ¦ Print		100
Print entire document	File ¦ Print		100
Exit EDIT	File ¦ Exit		100

■ REVIEW QUESTIONS

1. To toggle from Insert mode to Strikeover mode, press _____.
2. To quickly move the cursor to the end of the current line, press _____.
3. To quickly move the cursor to the beginning of the current line, press _____.
4. To copy selected text, execute _____ and after repositioning the cursor execute _____.
5. To move selected text, execute _____ and after repositioning the cursor execute _____.
6. To delete selected text, execute _____ or press _____.
7. When **O**pen is executed, only files with a(n) _____ extension are listed.
8. After editing an existing file, to save it so you have both your original and edited files on your disk, execute _____ from the File drop-down menu.
9. To clear the EDIT screen so you can start another document, execute _____ from the File drop-down menu.
10. EDIT (does/does not) _____ warn you when you attempt to exit without first saving a file.

■ *HANDS-ON EXERCISES*

Exercise 9-1 Boot your computer from drive C to the DOS prompt. If necessary, enter the usual startup PATH and PROMPT commands. Load DOSKEY. Insert your ACTIVITY disk into drive A. Change the current drive to drive A. Turn on the printer. Load EDIT.

Open the file CODING1.TXT in the ROOT directory on drive A. Make the following changes:

1. Type today's date on line 1 behind your name.
2. Delete the word "favorite" on line 4.
3. Replace "ASCII" with "ascii" on line 3.
4. Select lines 1 through 4 and print the selected text.
5. Copy the entire first line to line 6.
6. Move line 5 to line 2.
7. Print the entire document.
8. Save the document as CODES.TXT in the ROOT directory on drive A.

Exercise 9-2 Exit EDIT. Print a directory listing of the ROOT directory of drive A. Remove your printout. Turn off the printer, computer, and monitor. Remove your disk.

LESSON TEN: Customize Your System

OBJECTIVES

In this lesson you will learn how to:

- Determine the amount and type of memory.
- Use EDIT to create and change the AUTOEXEC.BAT and CONFIG.SYS files to customize your system.
- Hide commands being executed in a batch file.
- Include multiple directories in the PATH command.
- Use the Active Task List.
- Set undelete protection during booting.
- Set virus monitoring.

MEM (MEMORY)

Short for Memory, the MEM command displays a status report on the amount and type of memory a system has available. Several of the commands that you will work with in this lesson to customize your computer affect the amount of memory available for application programs.

To boot your computer:

1. Boot your computer from the hard drive. If necessary, enter the usual startup PATH and PROMPT commands. Load DOSKEY. Insert your ACTIVITY disk into drive A.
2. Turn on the printer.

To determine your computer's memory:

1. Type **mem** and press [Enter] to display a status report on your computer's memory.
2. Print the memory status report (**mem > prn**).
3. Remove your printout. If necessary, turn your printer on line. Later in this lesson you will use this printout to determine the effect on memory of commands that customize your computer.

103

AUTOEXEC.BAT

The AUTOEXEC.BAT file is one of two files used to customize a computer. The second file, CONFIG.SYS, is covered later in this lesson.

The AUTOEXEC.BAT file must be in the ROOT directory of the system disk used to boot a computer for the commands in it to be executed during the booting process. If any commands are added or changed in an existing AUTOEXEC.BAT file, the changes are not recognized by DOS until the file is executed again.

The BAT extension in the AUTOEXEC.BAT filename is DOS's shorthand for batch. A **batch file** is a holding file for DOS commands. The number of DOS commands that can be held in a batch file is unlimited. When a batch file is executed, DOS performs all the commands in the file.

To display the AUTOEXEC.BAT and CONFIG.SYS files on your hard drive:

1. Type **type c:\autoexec.bat** and press [Enter]. If "Bad command or file name" is displayed, your computer does not have an AUTOEXEC.BAT file.

2. If you have an AUTOEXEC.BAT file on your hard drive, type **type c:\autoexec.bat > prn** and press [Enter] to print a copy of the file.

3. Type **type c:\config.sys** and press [Enter]. If "Bad command or file name" is displayed, your computer does not have a CONFIG.SYS file.

4. If you do have a CONFIG.SYS file on your hard drive, print a copy of the file.

5. Remove your printout. If necessary, turn your printer on line.

To create an AUTOEXEC.BAT file:

1. Change the current drive to drive A.

2. Load the DOS Shell. If the Active Task List area is not visible, execute <u>E</u>nable Task Swapper from the Options drop-down menu.

3. Execute the IBM DOS Editor (MS-DOS Editor) command in the Main area of the DOS Shell.

4. Type **a:\autoexec.bat** and press [Enter] in the dialog box.

5. Type the following, pressing [Enter] after each line:

    date

    time

    path=c:\dos

    doskey

6. Execute <u>S</u>ave from the File drop-down menu.

Rather than exiting EDIT to test your AUTOEXEC.BAT file and then reloading it to make some changes, a program accessed in the DOS Shell can be temporarily exited by pressing [Ctrl]+[Esc]. The program will be listed in the Active Task List in the DOS Shell. Without returning to the DOS Shell, you can cycle through Active Task List programs to change to another open program by pressing [Alt]+[Tab]. All Active Task List programs must be exited before permanently exiting the DOS Shell.

To test your AUTOEXEC.BAT file without exiting EDIT:

1. Press [Ctrl]+[Esc] to temporarily exit EDIT to the DOS Shell. Notice that DOS Editor is listed in the Active Task List area.

2. Exit the DOS Shell temporarily (execute Command Prompt in the Main area).

3. Clear the screen (**cls**).

4. Execute your AUTOEXEC.BAT file by typing **autoexec** and pressing [Enter]

5. Press [Enter] to accept the current date and time displayed.

@ECHO OFF

As you look at your screen, all the commands you included in your AUTOEXEC.BAT file are displayed on the screen. The @ECHO OFF command is used in batch files to hide the commands being executed.

To return to EDIT to hide the commands being executed:

1. Press [Ctrl]+[Esc] to temporarily exit the DOS prompt to the DOS Shell.

2. Execute DOS Editor in the Active Task List area.

3. Insert **@echo off** and press [Enter] on line 1, position 1.

4. Execute **S**ave from the File drop-down menu.

To test your AUTOEXEC.BAT file:

1. Cycle through the open programs by holding down [Alt] and continually pressing [Tab] until Command Prompt is displayed at the top of your screen. Release both keys. You are at the DOS prompt.

NOTE: Some brands of IBM-compatible microcomputers will not cycle through all the open programs when [Alt]+[Tab] is used. Instead, you are returned to the DOS Shell. If this happens to you, execute the command in the Active Task List area to switch to the desired open program.

2. Clear the screen (**cls**).

3. Execute your AUTOEXEC.BAT file (**autoexec**).

4. Press Enter to accept the date and time displayed. All the commands are executed without being displayed on the screen.

5. Cycle through the open programs (Alt + Tab) to return to the DOS Editor.

PATH

Though you were introduced to the PATH command in Lesson Two, let's take a closer look at the command. The purpose of the PATH command is to allow DOS to execute a file with a BAT, COM, or EXE extension without including the directory path to the file as part of the command.

COM and EXE are extensions DOS uses to recognize programs. For instance, the file 123.EXE is used to load Lotus 1-2-3 and the file EDIT.COM is used to load EDIT. With the drive and directory path of the Lotus program included in your PATH command, you can start Lotus from any drive and directory by simply typing 123.

Multiple directories are separated by a semicolon (;) in the PATH command. Assume your word-processing program is stored in a directory named WP off the ROOT directory on drive C. The command PATH=C:\DOS;C:\WP sets a path to the DOS directory on drive C (C:\DOS) and to the WP directory on drive C (C:\WP). When entering the PATH command for multiple directories, do not leave a space before or after the semicolon separating the directory paths.

To include several directories in your PATH command:

1. Position your cursor at the end of the line with the PATH command.

2. Type **;a:\;a:\wordpro** so the line reads path=c:\dos;a:\;a:\wordpro.

3. Look at your earlier printout of the AUTOEXEC.BAT file on your hard drive. If one of the commands contains the word "mouse," position the cursor on the blank line below the last line in your file and type that command exactly as it appears on the printout.

4. Execute **S**ave.

To create files that test your multidirectory path:

1. Clear the screen to be able to start another document (File | **N**ew).

2. Type the following, pressing [Enter] at the end of each line:

   @echo off
   cls
   echo This batch file tests the path to WORDPRO

3. Execute Save. Type **a:\wordpro\test.bat** and press [Enter] in the Name: box.

4. Clear the screen to be able to start another document.

5. Type the following lines, pressing [Enter] at the end of each line:

   @echo off
   cls
   echo This file displays the contents of AUTOEXEC.BAT
   type a:\autoexec.bat

6. Execute Save. Type **a:\root.bat** and press [Enter] in the Name: box.

7. Execute Exit. As you exited EDIT using the Exit command, the DOS Editor is removed from the Active Task List in the DOS Shell.

To test your path to multiple directories:

1. Execute Command Prompt in the Active Task List area, highlight it, and press [Enter] or double-click on it to execute Command Prompt.

2. Execute your AUTOEXEC.BAT file (**autoexec**). Press [Enter] to accept the date and time displayed.

3. Change the current drive to drive C.

4. Type **test** and press [Enter]. The screen is cleared and the message "This batch file tests the path to WORDPRO" is displayed.

5. Type **root** and press [Enter]. The screen is cleared and the message "This file displays the contents of AUTOEXEC.BAT" is displayed followed by the lines in your AUTOEXEC.BAT file.

6. Type **exit** and press [Enter] to return to the DOS Shell. Command Prompt is no longer listed in the Active Task List as you returned to the DOS Shell by typing exit rather than using [Alt]+[Tab].

7. If you receive a screen message on MS-DOS Task Switcher support instead of returning to the DOS Shell, press [Ctrl]+[C] to return to the shell.

8. Permanently exit the DOS Shell.

You have just demonstrated that you can execute files with a BAT, COM, or EXE extension from any drive and directory as long as the entire path to the directory is included in the PATH command.

UNDELETE

Lesson Five mentioned that several levels of undelete protection are available. The easiest way to ensure that you have the level of protection you want is to set the undelete protection level during booting by including the appropriate command in your AUTOEXEC.BAT file.

To set the highest level of protection, Delete Sentry, use the command UNDELETE /S. To set the middle level of protection, Delete Tracker, use the command UNDELETE /T followed by the letter of the drive on which you want this level of protection, such as UNDELETE /TA for drive A or UNDELETE /TC for drive C. The Delete Tracker command is one of the few commands in which the drive letter is not followed by a colon. You can also enter either of the undelete protection commands at the DOS prompt.

COMPUTER VIRUSES

Computer viruses are unauthorized programs that produce a variety of negative effects on your computer. In general, virus programs are designed to replicate and spread, choking your system by becoming so large that your programs do not have room to run. Viruses may display random screen messages, produce unexpected sounds, and damage your disks and files.

DOS 6.0 has two virus detection alternatives. The command MSAV in your AUTOEXEC.BAT file loads an antivirus program to scan your computer's drives and memory each time you boot your computer. To continually monitor your system, the memory-resident program VSAFE can be included in your AUTOEXEC.BAT file or entered from the DOS prompt.

To set undelete and virus protection:

1. Use EDIT to modify your AUTOEXEC.BAT file (**edit a:\autoexec.bat**).

2. Position your cursor on the first blank line under the present lines in your file.

3. Type **undelete /ta** and press [Enter] to set the Delete Tracker level of protection for drive A.

4. Type **msav** and press [Enter] to check for viruses when AUTOEXEC.BAT is executed.

5. Type **vsafe** and press [Enter] so that your computer system is constantly monitored for virus activity.

6. Save your AUTOEXEC.BAT file and exit EDIT.

To test your AUTOEXEC.BAT file:

1. Clear the screen (**cls**).

2. Execute your AUTOEXEC.BAT file (**autoexec**).

3. Press [Enter] to accept the date and time displayed.

4. A dialog box for MSAV is displayed. Click on **Detect** or type **d** to scan memory and your disk in drive A for viruses.

5. After the virus scan is complete, a virus report is displayed. Press [Enter] or click on OK to return to the MSAV dialog box.

6. Type **x** or click on Exit to exit MSAV. Click on OK or press [Enter] to continue execution of your AUTOEXEC.BAT file. Notice the message telling you that VSAFE is loaded.

7. Do a directory listing of the file EGA.ABC in the ROOT directory on drive A, then delete it.

8. Do a directory listing of files starting with the letter E to confirm that EGA.ABC is deleted.

9. Undelete EGA.ABC (**undelete ega.abc**). With the Delete Tracker level of protection, you only need to confirm whether or not to undelete the file; you do not need to enter the first letter of the file being undeleted.

10. Determine the amount of memory available (**mem**). Compare the memory status report on the screen with the memory status report you printed at the beginning of this lesson.

CONFIG.SYS

During the booting process, DOS not only performs the commands in the AUTOEXEC.BAT file but also looks for a CONFIG.SYS file. As its name implies, the CONFIG.SYS file contains commands that configure or customize the environment, or resources, of your computer system.

Like AUTOEXEC.BAT, for the commands to be executed during booting the CONFIG.SYS file must be in the ROOT directory of the disk used to boot the computer. During booting DOS first executes commands in the CONFIG.SYS file to customize your computer's environment and then executes commands in the AUTOEXEC.BAT file. Therefore, any external commands included in the CONFIG.SYS file must include the complete directory path to the DOS directory.

DOS has over a dozen commands that can be included in the CONFIG.SYS file as well as several device driver commands to deal with disk drives, memory, and peripherals such as screens, keyboards, and printers.

To create a CONFIG.SYS file:

1. If necessary, change the current drive to drive A. ROOT should be the current directory.
2. Type **edit a:\config.sys** and press Enter
3. Type the following. Press Enter at the end of each line.

   break=on
   files=20
   buffers=15
   device=c:\dos\ansi.sys

4. If you have a mouse on your system and did not have a command in your AUTOEXEC.BAT file with the word "mouse," look at the printout of your CONFIG.SYS file on drive C. If one of the commands contains the word "mouse," type that command exactly as it appears on the printout.
5. Execute **S**ave and exit EDIT.

Before testing the CONFIG.SYS file you just created, let's take a quick look at the purpose of the commands you just typed.

BREAK

When DOS is executing a program, it only checks to see if you pressed Ctrl+C or Ctrl+Break (the cancel command) when the program requests **I/O (input or output)**. With the command BREAK=ON in the CONFIG.SYS file, DOS checks to see if you tried to cancel whenever the program requests any DOS function.

FILES

The FILES command controls the number of files that can be open concurrently. The default number of open files is 8. For some programs, however, this is insufficient. Windows 3.1, for instance, requires that you set the number of files that can be open concurrently to 30. The installation instructions of your application program tell you the number of files you need to open to use the program. You will want to set FILES to the largest number needed by any of your application programs.

BUFFERS

A **buffer** is a block of memory set aside to temporarily store I/O. Because reading or writing data to memory is faster than to disk, the BUFFERS command is DOS's attempt to increase the efficiency of programs by reducing the I/O time. The installation instructions of your application program will suggest the minimum number of buffers you need for the program to run in a timely fashion.

ANSI.SYS

The ANSI.SYS command is a device driver that is used to change the screen appearance and keyboard assignment. For instance, after booting with the ANSI.SYS command in the CONFIG.SYS file, you can change your screen color or the number of lines displayed on the screen.

To execute your CONFIG.SYS file:

1. Warm boot your computer ([Ctrl]+[Alt]+[Del]) with your ACTIVITY disk in drive A.

2. Accept or enter the current date and time when prompted. Exit the MSAV dialog box to the DOS prompt.

3. Type **mem > prn** and press [Enter]

4. Advance the paper and remove your printout. Compare this printout with your previous memory printout. Several of the CONFIG.SYS commands reduced the amount of memory available.

To use your ANSI.SYS driver:

1. Type **mode con: lines=50** and press [Enter]. This command sets the number of lines on your screen to 50.

2. Do a directory listing. Notice how small the text is and how close the lines are on your screen.

3. Type **mode con: lines=25** and press [Enter]. Now the number of lines on your screen is set to 25.

4. Do a directory listing. The lines are more widely spaced and the text is larger.

CUSTOMIZED BOOTING

When booting with DOS 6.0, you can bypass the AUTOEXEC.BAT and CONFIG.SYS files or confirm each line in the CONFIG.SYS file. When "Starting MS-DOS ..." is displayed, pressing [F5] boots without executing commands in the AUTOEXEC.BAT and CONFIG.SYS files. Pressing [F8] when "Starting MS-DOS ..." is displayed requires that you enter Y or N to confirm each line in the CONFIG.SYS file.

To bypass AUTOEXEC.BAT and CONFIG.SYS during booting:

1. With your ACTIVITY disk in drive A, warm boot your computer.
2. Press [F5] when "Starting MS-DOS ..." is displayed.
3. When you see the DOS prompt, display any paths in memory (**path**). As your AUTOEXEC.BAT file was not executed during booting, the message "No Path" is displayed.
4. Notice that the DOS prompt displays the current drive and directory.

To confirm commands in the CONFIG.SYS file during booting:

1. Warm boot your computer.
2. Press [F8] when "Starting MS-DOS ..." is displayed.
3. As each command in your CONFIG.SYS file is displayed, type y or n. When you enter y, the command is executed. When you enter n, the command is bypassed.

To turn off your computer:

1. Turn off your printer, computer, and monitor.
2. Remove your disk from drive A.

■ SUMMARY OF COMMANDS

Topic or Feature	Command or Key	Page
Display memory status report	MEM	103
Load EDIT from the DOS Shell	Main ¦ IBM or MS-DOS Editor	104
Temporarily exit a program to the DOS Shell	[Ctrl]+[Esc]	105
Cycle through active programs	[Alt]+[Tab]	105
Hide commands executed in a batch file	@ECHO OFF	105
Set paths to multiple directories into memory	PATH=C:\directory name;A:\directory name	106
Set Delete Sentry level of undelete protection	UNDELETE /S	108

Topic or Feature	Command or Key	Page
Set Delete Tracker level of undelete protection for drive A	UNDELETE /TA	108
Scan memory and drive for viruses during booting	MSAV	108
Continually monitor your system for viruses	VSAFE	108
Load EDIT and a file to be edited from the DOS prompt	EDIT A:\filename.ext	108
Check for cancel	BREAK=ON	110
Set number of files open concurrently	FILES=number	110
Set up temporary I/O storage	BUFFERS=number	110
Load screen and keyboard enhancer	DEVICE=C:\DOS\ANSI.SYS	110
Change number of lines on the screen	MODE CON: LINES=number	111
Bypass AUTOEXEC.BAT and CONFIG.SYS during booting	F5	112
Confirm CONFIG.SYS commands during booting	F8	112

■ REVIEW QUESTIONS

1. The IBM or MS-DOS Editor is a command listed in the _____ area of the DOS Shell.

2. In order to be executed during booting, both the CONFIG.SYS and AUTOEXEC.BAT files must be in the _____ directory of the disk used to boot the computer.

3. A(n) _____ is used to separate multiple directories included in the PATH command.

4. The command _____ hides the commands being executed in a batch file.

5. The _____ command displays a status report of memory.

6. The _____ command in the CONFIG.SYS file sets the maximum number of files that can be open concurrently.

7. The command _____ installs the Delete Tracker level of undelete protection on drive A.

8. To execute a file named TEST.BAT, you (do/do not) _____ need to type the extension.

9. To scan your system's memory and booting disk drive for viruses during booting, include the command _____ in your AUTOEXEC.BAT file.

10. Programs temporarily exited while using the DOS Shell are listed in the _____ area.

■ HANDS-ON EXERCISES

Exercise 10-1 With your ACTIVITY disk in drive A, boot your computer. Turn on the printer. Print a status report on the memory of your system. Access EDIT to change your CONFIG.SYS file in the ROOT directory on drive A. Change the number of files that can be open concurrently to 15. Print the complete document. Save the file and exit EDIT.

Exercise 10-2 Access EDIT to change your AUTOEXEC.BAT file in the ROOT directory on drive A. Change the file as necessary to have only the DOS directory on drive C and the ROOT directory on drive A in the PATH command. Print the complete document. Save the file and exit EDIT.

Exercise 10-3 Warm boot your computer with your ACTIVITY disk in drive A and bypass the AUTOEXEC.BAT and CONFIG.SYS files. Display the current path in memory. Enter a path to the DOS directory on drive C. Display a status report on the memory of your computer. Print the screen. Warm boot your computer with your ACTIVITY disk in drive A and confirm the execution of each command in the CONFIG.SYS file. Display the current path in memory. Display a status report on the memory of your computer. Print the screen. Remove your printout. Turn off your equipment. Remove your disk.

LESSON ELEVEN
Macros and Batch Files

OBJECTIVES

In this lesson you will learn how to:
- Access and use on-line HELP.
- Use DOSKEY to create a macro.
- Execute a macro.
- Display a list of macros in memory.
- Recognize when to use a REM or ECHO message in a batch file.
- Temporarily suspend execution of a batch file.

HELP

In addition to FASTHELP, which you learned to use in Lesson Two, DOS 6.0 also has on-line HELP. You can maneuver through on-line HELP from the keyboard or with a mouse. On-line HELP has more information available for commands than FASTHELP.

When HELP is entered from the DOS prompt, a HELP Command Reference screen like that shown in Figure 11-1 is displayed. The commands for which HELP is available are listed alphabetically. With a mouse, you click on the name of the command for which you want information. From the keyboard, [Tab], [Shift]+[Tab], [↑], and [↓] are used. Menu Bar items are accessed and commands selected from drop-down menus in the same manner as in the DOS Shell.

To boot your computer:

1. Boot your computer to the DOS prompt from the hard drive. Turn on the printer.

2. Insert your ACTIVITY disk into drive A. Change the current drive to drive A.

3. Execute your AUTOEXEC.BAT file on your ACTIVITY disk (**a:\autoexec**).

Figure 11-1
On-line Help Command Reference screen

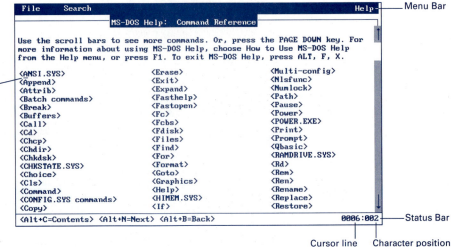

To access on-line HELP information:

1. Type **help** and press Enter. A screen similar to Figure 11-1 is displayed.

2. Follow the instructions at the top of the screen to view all of the commands for which HELP is available.

3. Type **d**. The cursor is positioned under the D of the Date command — the first command starting with the letter D.

4. Open Help in the Menu Bar. Execute the first command in the drop-down menu.

5. Execute <Navigating Through MS-DOS Help>.

You can scroll through the topics one-by-one by pressing Alt+N or clicking on the Next button in the Status Bar. To view a previous screen, press Alt+B or click on the Back button.

To scroll through the HELP topics:

1. Advance to the HELP information on the next topic (press Alt+N or click on the Next button in the Status Bar).

2. Return to the previous HELP topic (press Alt+B or click on the Back button in the Status Bar).

3. Return to the HELP Command Reference screen (press Alt+C or click on the Contents button in the Status Bar).

4. View the HELP information on the CLS command by clicking on <Cls> or by moving your cursor to it and then pressing Enter.

5. Return to the HELP Command Reference screen (Alt+C or the Contents button).

6. Exit HELP by executing Exit in the File drop-down menu.

To access HELP for an individual command, type **HELP** followed by the name of the command. Most commands have three HELP topic screens available—Syntax, Notes, and Examples. When you access HELP for an individual command, the Syntax topic screen is displayed.

To access the Notes or Examples topic screens, click on the <Notes> or <Examples> button at the top of the HELP screen. From the keyboard, type **N** or **E** to move the cursor to the <Notes> or <Examples> button and then press [Enter]

To access HELP for an individual command:

1. Type **help doskey** and press [Enter]. The Syntax topic screen for DOSKEY is displayed.

2. Display the Notes topic screen (type **n** and press [Enter] or click on the <Notes> button).

3. Return to the previous screen ([Alt]+[B] or Back button).

4. Display the Examples topic screen (click on the <Examples> button or type **e** and press [Enter]).

5. Open the File drop-down menu and execute the **P**rint command.

6. Return to the HELP Command Reference screen ([Alt]+[C] or Contents button).

7. Select <Xcopy> and explore the information available.

8. Open the File drop-down menu and execute Exit to return to the DOS prompt.

DOSKEY MACROS

Besides allowing you to edit previously entered commands, DOSKEY also lets you create and execute macros. A **macro** allows you to store several DOS commands to be executed in succession. The command(s) stored in a macro are executed by typing the macro name at the DOS prompt. As macros are stored in memory instead of on a disk, the macro is gone when the computer is turned off.

To create a macro with several commands, $T is typed between commands. The syntax to create a macro is:

DOSKEY MACRONAME=COMMAND $T COMMAND $T COMMAND

To create a macro:

1. Type **doskey drivec=c: $t cd \act** and press Enter

    You created a macro named DRIVEC that changes the current drive to drive C and then changes the current directory on drive C to ACT.

2. Type **doskey drivea=a: $t cd \wordpro $t dir /w** and press Enter

   You created another macro named DRIVEA that changes the current drive to drive A, changes the current directory on drive A to WORDPRO, and does a wide directory listing of the current directory.
   To execute a macro, just type the name of the macro. If you forget a macro name, type **DOSKEY /MACROS** to display all the macros in memory.

To execute a macro:

1. Type **drivec** and press Enter to execute the DRIVEC macro. The drive is immediately changed to drive C with ACT as the current directory.

2. Type **drivea** and press Enter. The drive is immediately changed to drive A with WORDPRO as the current directory and a wide directory listing of the files is displayed.

To list your macros:

1. Type **doskey /macros** and press Enter. Both macros that you created are listed.

2. Press F7 to see a numbered list of commands that you have entered. The complete commands to create both macros are included in the list.

3. Press F9 and type the line number of the command entered to create the DRIVEC macro. Press Enter

4. Type **$t tree** and press Enter at the end of the command. The command should read **doskey drivec=c: $t cd \act $t tree**.

5. Execute your DRIVEC macro. After changing to the ACT directory on drive C, the subdirectories of the ACT directory are listed.

BATCH FILES

In addition to macros, you can create batch files to do repetitive tasks. Batch files are saved to a disk while macros are temporary files in memory. Once a batch file is created and saved, it is available for use as long as the directory in which it is saved is included in the PATH command.

Batch files are powerful and useful files that enable execution of several commands by entering just one command. A batch file can contain DOS commands, the names of other batch files, and the name of an application program. The commands in a batch file are entered just as they are entered from the keyboard with each command on a separate line.

The BAT extension is always given to a batch file. Created using a text editor such as EDIT, a batch file is in ASCII, and the contents are readable using the TYPE command. To execute a batch file, all you do is type the filename. It is not necessary to include the BAT extension with the filename to execute the batch file.

Remember the PATH command you included in your AUTOEXEC.BAT file? DOS searches the current directory and every directory path named in the PATH command for any file that has a BAT, COM, or EXE extension.

When would you need a batch file? Any time you want to execute one or more commands automatically. Besides DOS commands, there are several special commands that can be included in a batch file.

REM (Remark)

The REM command allows a message to be displayed on the screen if @ECHO OFF has not been included earlier in the batch file. The message is helpful in reminding the user what the batch file is doing or telling the user of an action (switch disks or turn on the printer, for example) that should be done.

PAUSE

The PAUSE command halts the screen display, temporarily interrupting the execution of the batch file. The screen prompts the user with the message "Press any key to continue. . .". The user can continue or cancel execution of the batch file. The PAUSE command should be included in a batch file directly after the REM command to give the user time to read and act upon the REM message.

CREATE A BATCH FILE

The first step in creating a batch file is to list the task(s) that you want the batch file to do. The second step is to go through the tasks and write the command(s) for each task just as you would enter them from the keyboard. The last step is to create the batch file.

To create a batch file:

1. Change the current drive to drive A.

2. Change the current directory on drive A to the ROOT directory.

3. Type **edit a:\act.bat** and press Enter to load EDIT to create the ACT.BAT file. Type the following lines, pressing Enter at the end of each line.

   rem This batch file changes the current drive to drive c

   rem and the current directory on drive c to act.

   pause

   c:

   cd \act

4. Save this file and exit EDIT.

5. Clear the screen (**cls**).

To execute the batch file:

1. Type **act** and press Enter. The first two remarks are displayed and the message "Press any key to continue…" appears.

2. Press any key. The commands C: and CD \ACT are displayed as the current drive is changed to drive C and the current directory on drive C is changed to ACT.

ECHO

The previous screen display looks cluttered with the commands REM and PAUSE displayed. The DOS commands executed can be hidden by using the @ECHO OFF command. When @ECHO OFF is used as the first command, even the REM statements are also hidden. An ECHO message is used instead of REM to display statements when @ECHO OFF is the first command in a batch file. The advantage of entering a message behind ECHO is that only the message appears on the screen. The screen display is neat and easy to understand.

To edit your batch file:

1. Change the current drive to drive A.

2. Load EDIT to modify the ACT.BAT file.

3. On line 1, character 1, type **@echo off** and press Enter.

4. Edit lines 2 and 3 so they read:

   echo This batch file changes the current drive to drive c

   echo and the current directory on drive c to act.

5. Move your cursor to line 2, character 1. Type **cls** and press (Enter) to insert the command to clear the screen.

6. Save your file and exit EDIT.

To test your batch file:

1. Type **act** and press (Enter). The screen is cleared and the two lines of messages are displayed as well as the message of how to continue.

2. Press any key to continue. You are now in the ACT directory on drive C.

3. Change the current directory to DOS (**cd \dos**).

4. Type **act** and press (Enter) to execute your batch file.

5. Press any key to continue.

Your batch file can be executed from any drive and directory as your PATH command includes the directory containing the BAT file.

What if the user wants to cancel the batch file? The PAUSE command tells the user how to continue but not how to cancel. You can edit your batch file to include a message telling the user to press (Ctrl)+(C) to cancel.

To edit your batch file:

1. Change the current drive to drive A.

2. Load EDIT to modify your ACT.BAT file.

3. Edit your batch file so it looks like the following:

    @echo off

    cls

    echo This batch file changes the current drive to drive c

    echo and the current directory on drive c to act.

    echo To cancel press ctrl + c.

    pause

    c:

    cd \act

4. Save your batch file and exit EDIT.

To test your batch file:

1. Execute your ACT batch file.

2. Cancel your batch file following the instructions displayed in the message.

Many systems are set up with a menu to give the user a choice of which program should be loaded into memory. The following activity creates a simplified menu.

To create a menu:

1. Change the current drive to drive A with ROOT as the current directory.

2. Load EDIT to create a file named 1.BAT (**edit a:\1.bat**).

3. Enter the following lines in the file and then save the file:

   @echo off

   cls

   echo To display the directory structure of your disk

   pause

   **tree **

4. After saving your file, execute **New** in the File drop-down menu.

5. Enter the following lines in the file:

   @echo off

   cls

   echo This is a directory listing of the ACT directory on drive C

   pause

   dir c:\act /on /w

6. Execute **Save** and type **a:\2.bat** and press Enter to save the file as 2.BAT in the ROOT directory on drive A.

7. Execute **New** to clear the screen. Enter the following lines in the file and then save the file. Type **a:\3.bat** to save the file as 3.BAT in the ROOT directory of drive A.

   @echo off

   cls

   type a:\1.bat

   pause

   type a:\2.bat

   pause

   type a:\3.bat

8. Execute **New** to clear the screen. Enter the following lines starting on the line and position indicated: that is, 5,35 is line 5, position 35. Save the file, typing **a:\menu.txt** to save it in the ROOT directory of drive A. After typing the first line, the cursor returns to position 35. Press (Home) to move the cursor to position 1 and then press (→) to move to position 10. After typing the menu number, press (Tab) before typing the rest of the line.

   5,35 **Menu**

   10,10 **1**   **Display the directory structure of the current drive**

   13,10 **2**   **Display the files in the ACT directory on drive C**

   16,10 **3**   **Display the contents of these batch files**

   20,10 **Type 1, 2, or 3 and press Enter to perform the desired activity**

9. Execute **New** to clear the screen. Enter the following lines in the file and then save the file as MENU.BAT in the ROOT directory on drive A:

   @echo off

   cls

   type a:\menu.txt

10. Exit EDIT.

To test your menu:

1. Type **menu** and press (Enter) to execute your MENU.BAT file.
2. Select one of the menu choices.
3. Continue to execute your MENU.BAT file until you have tried all three choices.

To turn off your computer:

1. Turn off your computer and monitor.
2. Remove your disk.

■ SUMMARY OF COMMANDS

Topic or Feature	Command or Key	Page
Access on-line HELP Command Reference	HELP	116
Access on-line HELP for an individual command	HELP command	117

Topic or Feature	Command or Key	Page
Create a macro	DOSKEY macroname=	118
Separate multiple macro commands	$T	118
Execute a macro	macroname	118
List macros	DOSKEY /MACROS	118
Display a batch file message	REM	119
Temporarily halt execution of a batch file	PAUSE	119
Hide batch file commands being executed	@ECHO OFF	120
Display a batch file message with @ECHO OFF	ECHO message	120

■ REVIEW QUESTIONS

1. To access on-line HELP for the DIR command, enter _____ at the DOS prompt.
2. When creating a macro, _____ is used between commands.
3. When macros are created, they are (permanent/temporary) _____ files stored (to disk/in memory) _____.
4. To display a listing of macros, enter the command _____.
5. To execute a macro named DRIVEC, at the DOS prompt type _____.
6. To temporarily halt the execution of a batch file so the user can read a screen message, use the _____ command.
7. To execute a batch file named ACT, at the DOS prompt type _____.
8. If all the commands are displayed as they are executed in a batch file, use _____ to display a message to the user; if none of the commands are displayed as they are executed, use _____ to display a message to the user.

9. In order for a batch file to be executed from any drive and directory, the directory where the batch file is saved must be included in the _____ command.

10. The _____ extension is always used for batch files.

■ HANDS-ON EXERCISES

Exercise 11-1   Boot your computer to the DOS prompt with your ACTIVITY disk in drive A. Turn on the printer. Access on-line HELP for the XCOPY command. Print the <Examples> topic information. Access the HELP Command Reference screen and look at the information for the DIR command. Print the <Notes> topic information. Exit the on-line HELP to the DOS prompt.

Exercise 11-2   Load EDIT to modify the file MENU.TXT. On line 19 add a fourth choice to the menu that does a directory listing of all the files with a BAT extension in the ROOT directory of drive A. After saving the file, use EDIT to create the file 4.BAT, which performs the activity you just added to the menu. Save the 4.BAT file to the ROOT directory on drive A. Exit EDIT. Execute your MENU.BAT file and select choice 4. Print the screen.

Exercise 11-3   Create a macro named LESSON11 that copies all files with a BAT extension in the ROOT directory of drive A to the WORDPRO directory (off ROOT) on drive A and then does a wide directory listing of WORDPRO. Execute your macro. Print the screen. Print an unnumbered list of all the commands entered since you booted your computer. Remove your printout. Turn off your equipment. Remove your disk.

LESSON TWELVE Advanced Commands

OBJECTIVES

In this lesson you will learn how to:

- Customize the DOS Shell by associating files.
- Customize the DOS Shell by adding program groups.
- Create program items for a program group.
- Determine your systems hardware configuration.
- Create and use a menu in the CONFIG.SYS file.

ASSOCIATE FILES

Data files can be associated with specific application programs via the filename extension. Most application programs automatically assign an extension to the name of a file. By associating data files with specific programs, you can start your application program in the DOS Shell by executing (double-click or highlight and press Enter) the name of the data file in the File List area. The directory containing the application program must be included in the PATH command in your AUTOEXEC.BAT file.

Though EDIT does not automatically assign an extension to a filename, only files with a TXT extension are listed when you load a file using Open in the File drop-down menu. You can associate files with a TXT extension to EDIT so that you can load EDIT by executing the data filename. Figure 12-1 shows the dialog box associating TXT files with EDIT.

Figure 12-1
Associate file dialog box

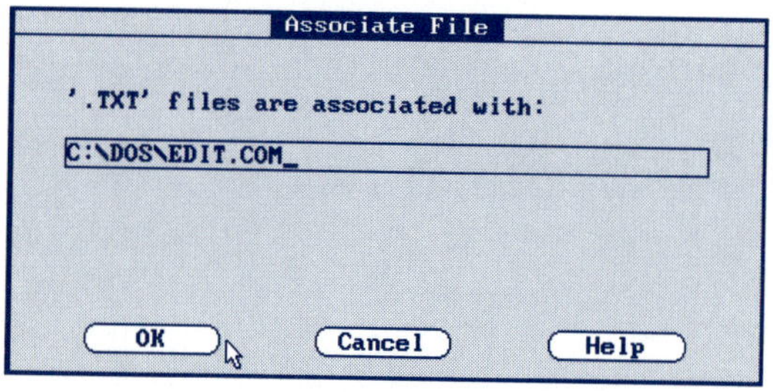

To boot your computer:

1. Boot your computer from the hard drive to the DOS prompt. Insert your ACTIVITY disk into drive A. Change the current drive to drive A.

2. Execute the AUTOEXEC.BAT file on your ACTIVITY disk (**a:\autoexec**).

3. Copy MENU.TXT to the ROOT directory on drive A with the name TEST.ASC (**copy menu.txt test.asc**).

4. Access the DOS Shell.

To associate files:

1. Highlight MENU.TXT in the ROOT directory on drive A.

2. Open the File drop-down menu and execute Associate.

The cursor is blinking in the parameters box for you to type the entire directory path and filename that starts the program to be associated with the highlighted file.

3. Type **c:\dos\edit.com** in the parameters box and then click on OK or press (Enter) to set the association.

To test the file association:

1. Execute MENU.TXT in the ROOT directory on drive A (double-click on the file or highlight the file and press (Enter)). EDIT is loaded and the MENU.TXT file is displayed.

2. Exit EDIT.

To remove the file association:

1. Highlight MENU.TXT in the ROOT directory on drive A. A file with the associated extension must be highlighted in order to remove the association.

2. Execute Associate from the File drop-down menu.

3. Press (Backspace) to remove all the text in the parameters box.

4. Click on OK or press (Enter)

5. Execute MENU.TXT (double-click or highlight and press (Enter)). Nothing happens as the file association has been removed.

If an application program assigns multiple extensions based on the type of file created, you can associate multiple extensions to the application program. For instance, WK1 and PIC are the extensions that Lotus 1-2-3 automatically assigns to spreadsheet and graph files, respectively. Figure 12-2 shows the dialog box with WK1 and PIC associated with Lotus 1-2-3. Associating several extensions to an application program allows you to load the program by executing any of the files created by it.

Figure 12-2
Associate file dialog box with multiple extensions

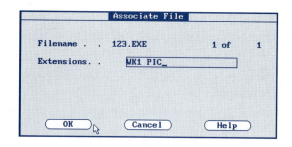

To associate multiple extensions:

1. Change the current drive to drive C (Ctrl+C).
2. Highlight DOS in the Directory Tree.
3. Scroll through the files in the File List area to highlight EDIT.COM.
4. With EDIT.COM highlighted, execute Associate in the File drop-down menu. The cursor is positioned in the parameters box.
5. Type **asc txt** in the parameters box and then press Enter

To test the multiple extensions:

1. Change the current drive to drive A.
2. Execute MENU.TXT in the ROOT directory on drive A. EDIT is loaded and the contents of MENU.TXT appear on the EDIT screen.
3. Exit EDIT.
4. Execute TEST.ASC in the ROOT directory on drive A. EDIT is again loaded with the contents of TEST.ASC available for editing.
5. Exit EDIT.

To remove the association with multiple extensions:

1. Change the current drive to drive C.
2. Highlight EDIT.COM in the DOS directory.
3. Execute Associate in the File drop-down menu.
4. Press Backspace until you have erased all the text in the parameters box and then close the dialog box by clicking on OK or pressing Enter
5. Change the current drive to drive A.
6. Execute MENU.TXT in the ROOT directory. Nothing happens as the file association was removed.
7. Execute TEST.ASC in the ROOT directory. Again, nothing happens as the file association was removed.

PROGRAM GROUPS AND ITEMS

If you share your computer with several other users, you might organize your hard drive so that each user's data files are kept in a separate directory. The DOS Shell can be customized to make it easy for each user to work with his or her own data files by creating a separate program group for each user in the Main area of the DOS Shell.

To set up a program group:

1. Highlight the Main area heading in the DOS Shell.

2. Execute New in the File drop-down menu. The New Program Object dialog box gives you a choice of creating a new program group or program item.

3. Click in the Program Group button or press [↑] once to fill the button in front of Program Group and then press [Enter] or click on OK.

4. Type **NEW GROUP** in the Title box.

5. Press [Enter] or click on OK. You are immediately returned to the DOS Shell. The title NEW GROUP is listed in the Main area.

Once a new program group is added, the next step is to add program items to it. If you use several application programs, you might customize the DOS Shell by adding a program item for each program. When a program item is executed, it automatically changes the startup directory to the directory containing the data files and loads the application program. The Add Program dialog box in Figure 12-3 has information typed in for several of the items.

Figure 12-3
Add Program dialog box

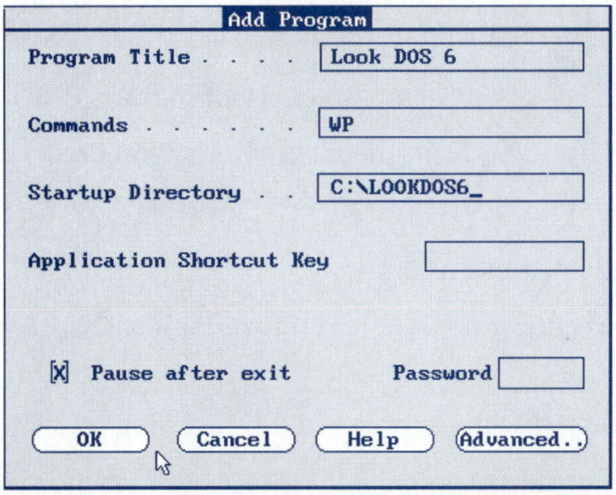

The Program Title in Figure 12-3, Look DOS 6, will appear in the program list. In the Commands box, WP is the command that starts the program. Because the directory containing the WP.EXE file is included in the PATH command in the AUTOEXEC.BAT file, the complete path to the file is not included. The Startup Directory specifies that when this program item is executed, DOS Shell changes the current directory to LOOKDOS6 on drive C. This is the directory containing all the lessons for this text.

> **CAUTION: When entering the items in the Add Program dialog box, press [Tab] or [↓] to move to the next item. If you press [Enter], the dialog box is exited and you are returned to the DOS Shell.**

To set up program items:

1. Execute NEW GROUP in the Main area (double-click on it or highlight and press [Enter]). Now the heading shows NEW GROUP instead of Main.

2. Execute New in the File drop-down menu.

3. Because the button in front of Program Item is filled, press [Enter] or click on OK.

4. Type your first name in the Program Title box. Press [↓]

5. Type **EDIT** in the Commands box. Press [↓]

6. Type **C:\ACT** in the Startup Directory box.

7. Click on OK or press [Enter]. Your first name is shown as an item in the NEW GROUP.

8. To add another program item to NEW GROUP:

    a. Execute New in the File drop-down menu.

    b. As the Program Item button is filled, press [Enter] or click on OK.

    c. Type your last name in the Program Title box. Press [↓]

    d. Type **EDIT** in the Commands box. Press [↓]

    e. Type **A:** in the Startup Directory box. Click on OK or press [Enter]

To use the program items:

1. Execute your last name (double-click on it or highlight it and press [Enter]).

2. Press [Esc] to remove the EDIT dialog box. EDIT is loaded.

3. Execute Open in the File drop-down menu. You can see that the startup directory is changed to list TXT files in the ROOT directory on drive A.

4. Cancel the file listing to return to the EDIT screen.

5. Exit EDIT to the DOS Shell.

6. Execute your first name. Press [Esc] to remove the EDIT dialog box.

7. Execute Open in the File drop-down menu. You can see that the startup directory is changed to list TXT files in C:\ACT.

8. Cancel the file listing to return to the EDIT screen.

9. Exit EDIT to the DOS Shell.

To change a program item title:

1. Highlight your last name in NEW GROUP.

2. Execute Properties in the File drop-down menu.

3. Type **CLASS WORK** in the Program Title box. Click on OK or press Enter. The change in the program item title is immediately shown in the NEW GROUP list.

To remove a program item and group:

1. Highlight your first name in NEW GROUP.

2. Execute Delete from the File drop-down menu. The dialog box gives you a choice of whether or not to delete this item.

3. With "Delete this item" highlighted, click on OK or press Enter. Your first name is removed as a program item.

4. Highlight CLASS WORK in NEW GROUP.

5. Remove CLASS WORK by pressing Del. Press Enter or click on OK in the dialog box that appears.

6. Execute Main in NEW GROUP. Main is now listed as the area title, and NEW GROUP is listed as one of the program groups that can be selected.

7. If necessary, highlight NEW GROUP and then press Del to remove it.

MSD (MICROSOFT DIAGNOSTICS)

The MSD command in DOS 6.0 displays technical information about your computer system. An informational screen similar to Figure 12-4 is displayed when you execute MSD. You can examine the information in more detail by clicking on the desired MSD button on the screen or by typing the letter highlighted in the button.

To use MSD:

1. Permanently exit the DOS Shell (press F3).

2. Type **msd** and press Enter. An informational screen similar to Figure 12-4 is displayed.

Figure 12-4
MSD screen

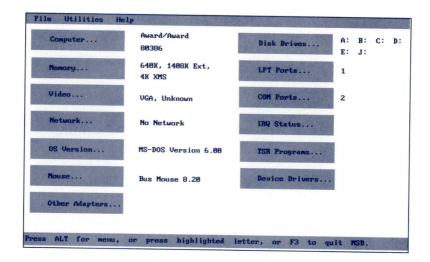

3. To view information about your operating system, click on the OS Version button or type **o** (the highlighted letter).

4. Click on OK or press Enter to close the Operating System Version screen.

5. Click on the **D**isk Drives button or type **d** to view information about your system's disk drives.

6. Close the Disk Drives screen (click on OK or press Enter).

7. Press F3 to exit the MSD screen.

CONFIG.SYS MENU

In Lesson Ten, you created a CONFIG.SYS file on your ACTIVITY disk. With DOS 6.0 you can create a menu in your CONFIG.SYS file to define several system configurations for multiple users.

To define several configurations:

1. If necessary, change the current drive to drive A with ROOT as the current directory.

2. To save the CONFIG.SYS file you created in Lesson Ten, rename CONFIG.SYS to CONFIG.OLD (**ren config.sys config.old**).

3. Load EDIT to create CONFIG.SYS (**edit config.sys**).

4. Type the following:

Lesson 12/Advanced Commands

[menu]
menuitem=Jack
menuitem=Mary
menucolor=4,7

[common]
files=30

[Jack]
buffers=30
numlock=off

[Mary]
buffers=20

5. Save the file.

6. Exit EDIT.

This CONFIG.SYS file configures the computer for either Jack or Mary. The menu displayed during booting is in red (4 in the menucolor command) on a white background (7 in the menucolor command). FILES=30 in the first (common) section is executed for both configurations.

When the menu is displayed during booting, you can select whether to execute the configuration commands for Jack or Mary. When Jack is selected, 30 blocks of memory are set aside for temporary input/output storage and NumLock is toggled off. When Mary is selected, the buffers are set to 20.

To test your CONFIG.SYS file:

1. With your ACTIVITY disk in drive A, warm boot your computer ([Ctrl]+[Alt]+[Del]). The MS-DOS 6 Startup Menu displays 1 for Jack and 2 for Mary.

2. Type **1** and press [Enter] to execute the configuration commands for Jack.

3. When the DOS prompt is displayed, notice that the NumLock light is off.

4. Warm boot your computer. Notice that at the bottom of the menu screen DOS 6.0 displays how to bypass the AUTOEXEC.BAT and CONFIG.SYS files or how to confirm each line in the CONFIG.SYS file.

5. Type **2** and press [Enter] to execute the configuration commands for Mary.

6. When the DOS prompt is displayed, notice that the NumLock light is on.

To turn off your computer:

1. Turn off your computer and monitor.

2. Remove your ACTIVITY disk from drive A.

■ SUMMARY OF COMMANDS

Topic or Feature	Command or Key	Shortcut	Page
Associate files with an application program	File |Associate		127
Create a program group	File |New |Program Group		129
Create a program item	File |New |Program Item		130
Delete a program group	File |Delete	Del	131
Change a program item	File |Properties		131
Delete a program item	File |Delete	Del	131
Display technical information about your computer system	MSD		131
Create a menu in CONFIG.SYS	[MENU]		133
Create CONFIG.SYS menu items	MENUITEM=name		133
Set up startup menu colors	MENUCOLOR= number,number		133
Create section to enter CONFIG.SYS commands to be executed for all menu items	[COMMON]		133
Set NumLock off	NUMLOCK=OFF		133

■ REVIEW QUESTIONS

1. In order to start an application program by executing a filename, the _____ of the data filename must be associated with the program.

2. To remove an extension from being associated with an application program, highlight a filename with the extension to be removed before executing _____ in the File drop-down menu.

3. A new program group is created by executing _____ in the File drop-down menu.

4. To change the name of a program item, execute _____ in the File drop-down menu after first highlighting the program item to be changed.

5. When setting up a program item for each user, you (can/cannot) _____ change the drive and directory.

6. To remove a program item, after highlighting the program item name, execute _____ in the File drop-down menu or press _____.

7. To display technical information about your computer system, type _____ at the DOS prompt.

8. To boot with the NumLock off, type _____ in the CONFIG.SYS file.

9. Commands in the CONFIG.SYS file that are to be executed for all of the configurations are listed in the _____ section.

10. To create Class as an item in the DOS Startup Menu, the command _____ is entered in the CONFIG.SYS file.

■ HANDS-ON EXERCISES

Exercise 12-1

Boot your computer from drive C to the DOS prompt. Turn on the printer. Insert your ACTIVITY disk into drive A. Change the current drive to drive A. Execute the AUTOEXEC.BAT file on your ACTIVITY disk. Access the DOS Shell. Create LESSON 12 as a program group in the Main area. Execute LESSON 12. Highlight LESSON 12 to create a program item. Enter EXERCISE in the Title box, EDIT for the Command, and A:\ as the Startup Directory.

Execute EXERCISE. Press [Esc] to remove the EDIT dialog box. Type the following line:

I used a program item to load EDIT.

Print the file. Save the file with the name CLASS.TXT and exit EDIT. Highlight EXERCISE and then remove it as a program item. Execute Main. Highlight LESSON 12 and then remove it as a program group.

Exercise 12-2

Select the File List heading and refresh your screen. Highlight CLASS.TXT in the ROOT directory on drive A and associate it with EDIT.COM in the DOS directory on drive C. After completing the association, execute CLASS.TXT. Insert your first and last name on line 2. Save the file. Print the file and exit EDIT. Remove the association. Permanently exit the DOS Shell. Remove your printout. Turn off your equipment. Remove your disk.

Answers to Review Questions

LESSON 1

1. C
2. cold
3. warm
4. [Shift]
5. toggle
6. CLS
7. do not
8. [Ctrl]+[C] or [Ctrl]+[Break]
9. [Ctrl]+[Alt]+[Del]
10. TIME

LESSON 2

1. > PRN
2. DATE /? or FASTHELP DATE
3. C, ROOT
4. backslash (\)
5. Internal
6. external
7. PATH=C:\DOS
8. PROMPT PG
9. terminate-and-stay-resident (TSR)
10. [F7]

LESSON 3

1. system
2. external
3. FORMAT A: /S
4. FORMAT A: /S /F:720
5. thousand
6. million
7. DIR
8. DIR C:
9. C:
10. felt-tip pen

LESSON 4

1. ROOT
2. parent, subdirectory
3. TREE
4. DIR ..
5. CD C:
6. MD TRAVEL
7. CD \
8. CD TEMP
9. DELTREE TRAVEL
10. CD ..

LESSON 5

1. COPY C:OLD.TXT A:
2. COPY C:OLD.TXT A:NEW.TXT
3. MOVE OLD.TXT PRACTICE or MOVE A:OLD.TXT A:PRACTICE
4. EDIT A:\NEW.TXT
5. [Alt]+[F], S (Save)
6. TYPE NEW.TXT
7. REN OLD.TXT NEW.TXT
8. DEL BUDGET.WP
9. DEL *.*
10. UNDELETE

LESSON 6

1. cannot
2. cannot
3. can
4. XCOPY A:\ C:\PRACTICE /S
5. /S
6. CHKDSK
7. CHKDSK A:*.*
8. fragmented
9. DEFRAG A:
10. SYS A:

LESSON 7

1. DOSSHELL
2. Directory Tree
3. changes
4. click, [Alt]+[F]
5. is not
6. dialog box
7. does
8. E<u>x</u>it, [F3] or [Alt]+[F4]
9. **Exit**
10. [+]

LESSON 8

1. Disk Utilities
2. cannot
3. [Del]
4. [F8]
5. do
6. [F7]
7. [Alt]
8. [F5]
9. <u>R</u>un
10. cannot, can

LESSON 9

1. [Ins]
2. [End]
3. [Home]
4. **Copy, Paste**
5. **Cut, Paste**
6. **Clear,** [Del]
7. TXT
8. Save **As**
9. New
10. does

LESSON 10

1. Main
2. ROOT
3. semicolon (;)
4. @ECHO OFF
5. MEM
6. FILES
7. UNDELETE /TA
8. do not
9. MSAV
10. Active Task List

LESSON 11

1. HELP DIR
2. $T
3. temporary, in memory
4. DOSKEY /MACROS
5. **Drivec**
6. PAUSE
7. **Act**
8. REM, ECHO
9. PATH
11. BAT

LESSON 12

1. extension
2. <u>A</u>ssociate
3. <u>N</u>ew
4. <u>P</u>roperties
5. can
6. Delete, [Del]
7. MSD
8. NUMLOCK=OFF
9. [COMMON]
10. MENUITEM=CLASS

Answers to Hands-On Exercises

LESSON 1

1-1. C:\>TIME
      C:\>time
      C:\>Time
      C:\>DATE
      C:\>date
      C:\>Date

1-2. [Ctrl]+[Alt]+[Del]
      [Ctrl]+[Print Screen]
      [Enter]
      C:\>DIR [Enter]+[Ctrl]+[S] or [Pause]
      C:\>DIR [Enter]+[Ctrl]+[C] or [Ctrl]+[Break]
      C:\>CLS
      [Ctrl]+[Print Screen]
      [Enter]

LESSON 2

2-1. C:\>PATH
      C:\>PATH=C:\DOS
      C:\>PROMPT PG
      C:\>DOSKEY
      C:\>FASTHELP
      C:\>FASTHELP PROMPT or PROMPT /?
      C:\>FASTHELP DOSKEY or DOSKEY /?
      C:\>FASTHELP DATE or DATE /?
      C:\>FASTHELP PATH or PATH /?
      C:\>FASTHELP CLS or CLS /?
      C:\>FASTHELP TIME or TIME /?
      C:\>FASTHELP FASTHELP or FASTHELP /?

2-2. 1. C:\> [Page Up]
      2. C:\> [Page Down]
      3. C:\>P [F8]
      4. C:\> [F9] 4
      5. C:\> [F7]
      6. C:\>DOSKEY /HISTORY
      C:\>DOSKEY /HISTORY > PRN

LESSON 3

3-1. C:\>PATH=C:\DOS
      C:\>PROMPT PG
      C:\>DOSKEY
      C:\>FORMAT A: first name
      [Print Screen] or [Shift]+[Print Screen]
      C:\>FORMAT A: /S last name
      [Print Screen] or [Shift]+[Print Screen]

3-2. [Ctrl]+[Print Screen]
      [Enter]
      1. C:\>DIR /W
      2. C:\>DIR /ON
      3. C:\>DIR /P
      4. C:\>DIR /OE /W
      5. C:\>DIR /OD
      6. C:\>DIR /AH
      C:\>A:
      1. A:\>DIR C: /W
      2. A:\>DIR C: /ON
      3. A:\>DIR C: /P
      4. A:\>DIR C: /OE /W
      5. A:\>DIR C: /OD
      6. A:\>DIR C: /AH
      A:\>DOSKEY /HISTORY
      [Ctrl]+[Print Screen]
      [Enter]

LESSON 4

4-1. [Ctrl]+[Print Screen]
      [Enter]
      C:\>PATH=C:\DOS
      C:\>PROMPT PG
      C:\>DOSKEY
      C:\>CD DOS
      1. C:\DOS>DIR D*.*
      2. C:\DOS>DIR *.EXE
      3. C:\DOS>DIR ?O??.*

C:\DOS>A:
1. A:\>DIR C:D*.*
2. A:\>DIR C:*.EXE
3. A:\>DIR C:?O??.*

4-2.
1. A:\>MD LESSON
2. A:\>CD LESSON
   A:\LESSON>MD EXERCISE
3. A:\LESSON>CD \
   A:\>MD TESTDIR
4. A:\>CD TESTDIR
   A:\TESTDIR>MD PRACTICE
A:\TESTDIR>CD \
A:\>TREE
A:\>CD TESTDIR\PRACTICE
1. A:\TESTDIR\PRACTICE>DIR ..
2. A:\TESTDIR\PRACTICE>DIR \
3. A:\TESTDIR\PRACTICE>DIR \LESSON
A:\TESTDIR\PRACTICE>CD ..
1. A:\TESTDIR>DIR PRACTICE
2. A:\TESTDIR>DIR .. or DIR \
3. A:\TESTDIR>DIR \LESSON
A:\TESTDIR>RD PRACTICE
A:\TESTDIR>CD .. or CD \
A:\>TREE
A:\>RD TESTDIR
A:\>DELTREE LESSON
A:\>DIR
A:\>DOSKEY /HISTORY

LESSON 5

5-1. C:\>PATH=C:\DOS
C:\>PROMPT PG
C:\>DOSKEY
C:\>A:
A:\>EDIT A:\PRAC.TXT [Enter]
Type file lines
[Alt]+[F]   S (Save)
[Alt]+[F]   X (Exit)
[Ctrl]+[Print Screen]
[Enter]

5-2.
1. A:\>COPY PRAC.TXT TRAVEL
2. A:\>TYPE PRAC.TXT
3. A:\>REN PRAC.TXT PRACTICE.TXT
4. A:\>CD TRAVEL
5. A:\TRAVEL>DEL PRAC.TXT
6. A:\TRAVEL>UNDELETE PRAC.TXT
7. A:\TRAVEL>MOVE PRAC.TXT \
8. A:\TRAVEL>CD \

9. A:\>TREE /F
10. A:\>DOSKEY /HISTORY
[Ctrl]+[Print Screen]
[Enter]

LESSON 6

6-1. A:\>PATH=C:\DOS;C:\
A:\>DOSKEY
[Ctrl]+[Print Screen]
[Enter]
A:\>DISKCOPY A: A:
A:\>TREE /F

6-2. A:\>C:
C:\>SYS A:
C:\>CD ACT\WORDPRO
C:\ACT\WORDPRO>XCOPY C: A:\LESSON6 /S /E

6-3. C:\ACT\WORDPRO>A:
A:\>TREE /F
A:\>CHKDSK *.*
A:\>DEFRAG A:
A:\>DOSKEY /HISTORY
[Ctrl]+[Print Screen]
[Enter]

LESSON 7

7-1. C:\>PATH=C:\DOS
C:\>PROMPT= PG
C:\>DOSKEY
C:\>DOSSHELL
[*] [+] [−] [Ctrl]+[*]
Tree drop-down menu commands
[Ctrl]+[A]
Main |Command Prompt
A:\>**exit**
[Ctrl]+[C]

7-2. Options |File Display Options
1. *.EXE, size button filled
2. D*.* X in Descending Order brackets, extension button filled
3. *.* Remove X in Descending Order, name button filled
View |Dual File Lists
View |Program/File Lists
[Ctrl]+[A]
File |Exit or [Alt]+[F4] or [F3]

LESSON 8

8-1. C:\>PATH=C:\DOS
C:\>PROMPT PG
C:\>DOSKEY
C:\>DOSSHELL
Main ¦ Disk Utilities ¦ Format
A: /s PRAC8
[Ctrl]+[A]
Directory Tree
1. [Alt]+File
   Create Directory TESTDIR
   Select TESTDIR
2. [Alt]+File
   Create Directory PRACTICE

8-2. View ¦ Dual File Lists
1. Highlight EGA.ABC
   File ¦ Copy or [F8] or drag
2. Highlight TAG.EXE
   File ¦ Copy or [F8] or drag
3. Highlight EGA.ABC
   File ¦ Copy or [F8] or drag
   File ¦ Run TREE A:\ /F > PRN

8-3. View ¦ Program/File Lists
[Ctrl]+[A]
1. Highlight PRACTICE directory
   Highlight EGA.ABC
   File ¦ Move or [F7] or [Alt]+drag
2. Highlight PRACTICE, press [Del]
3. Highlight TESTDIR
   File ¦ Rename LESSON8
4. File ¦ Exit or [Alt]+[F4] or [F3]
   A:\LESSON8>CD \
   A:\>TREE /F > PRN

LESSON 9

9-1. C:\>PATH=C:\DOS
C:\>PROMPT PG
C:\>DOSKEY
C:\>A:
A:\>EDIT [Esc]
File ¦ Open CODING1.TXT
1. Press [End], type the current date
2. Select favorite, press [Del]
3. Press [Ins], type ascii
4. Press [Ins], select lines
   File ¦ Print
5. Select line   Edit ¦ Copy
   Set cursor   Edit ¦ Paste
6. Select line   Edit ¦ Cut
   Set cursor   Edit ¦ Paste
7. File ¦ Print
8. File ¦ Save As CODES.TXT

9-2. File ¦ Exit
DIR > PRN

LESSON 10

10-1. A:\>MEM > PRN
A:\>EDIT A:\CONFIG.SYS
Edit line to read FILES=15
[Alt]+[F]   P (Print)
[Alt]+[F]   S (Save)
[Alt]+[F]   X (Exit)

10-2. A:\>EDIT A:\AUTOEXEC.BAT
The PATH command should read
    PATH=C:\DOS;A:\
[Alt]+[F]   P (Print)
[Alt]+[F]   S (Save)
[Alt]+[F]   X (Exit)

10-3. [Ctrl]+[Alt]+[Del]
[F5]
A:\>PATH
A:\>PATH=C:\DOS
A:\>MEM
[Print Screen] or [Shift]+[Print Screen]
[Ctrl]+[Alt]+[Del]
[F8]
A:\>PATH
A:\>MEM
[Print Screen] or [Shift]+[Print Screen]

LESSON 11

11-1. A:\>HELP XCOPY
<Examples> or **E**
File ¦ Print
[Alt]+[C] or Contents button
<DIR>
<Notes> or [N]
File ¦ Print
File ¦ Exit

11-2. A:\>EDIT A:\MENU.TXT
　　　 Insert 4　**Do a DIR of batch files**
　　　 [Alt]+[F]　S (Save)
　　　 [Alt]+[F]　N (New)
　　　 @ECHO OFF
　　　 DIR A:*.BAT
　　　 [Alt]+[F]　S (Save) enter A:\4.BAT as filename
　　　 [Alt]+[F]　X (Exit)
　　　 A:\>MENU
　　　 A:\>4
　　　 [Print Screen] or [Shift]+[Print Screen]

11-3. A:\>DOSKEY LESSON11=COPY A:*.BAT
　　　　A:\WORDPRO $T DIR A:\WORDPRO /W
　　　 A:\>LESSON11
　　　 [Print Screen] or [Shift]+[Print Screen]
　　　 A:\>DOSKEY /HISTORY > PRN

LESSON 12

12-1. C:\>A:
　　　 A:\>AUTOEXEC
　　　 A:\>DOSSHELL
　　　 Select Main
　　　 File ¦ New ¦ Program Group
　　　 Lesson 12
　　　 Execute LESSON 12
　　　 File ¦ New ¦ Program Item
　　　 Exercise
　　　 EDIT
　　　 A:\
　　　 Execute EXERCISE
　　　 [Esc]
　　　 Type text
　　　 File ¦ Print
　　　 File ¦ Save CLASS.TXT
　　　 File ¦ Exit
　　　 Select EXERCISE
　　　 File ¦ Delete or [Del]
　　　 Execute Main
　　　 Select LESSON 12
　　　 File ¦ Delete or [Del]

12-2. [F5]
　　　 Select CLASS.TXT
　　　 File ¦ Associate
　　　 C:\DOS\EDIT.COM
　　　 Execute CLASS.TXT
　　　 Type text
　　　 File ¦ Save
　　　 File ¦ Print
　　　 File ¦ Exit
　　　 Select CLASS.TXT
　　　 File ¦ Associate
　　　 [Backspace] to remove association
　　　 File ¦ Exit or [Alt]+[F4] or [F3]

DOS 6.0 Command Summary

Commands without page numbers are not covered in this book.

Topic or Feature	Command	Page
Backs up and restores files.	MSBACKUP	
Calls one batch program from another.	CALL	
Changes the appearance of the DOS prompt.	PROMPT	14
Changes the terminal device used to control your system.	CTTY	
Checks a disk for file integrity and displays a status report.	CHKDSK	62
Checks for a processing condition.	IF	
Clears the screen.	CLS	5
Compares two files or sets of files and displays differences.	FC	
Compares two floppy disks.	DISKCOMP	
Compresses files on a disk.	DBLSPACE	
Configures a hard disk for use.	FDISK	
Configures a keyboard for a specific language.	KEYB	
Configures a system device.	MODE	
Connects two computers.	INTERLINK	
Converts .EXE files to binary.	EXE2BIN	
Copies file(s).	COPY	46
Copies files (except hidden and system files) and directory structure.	XCOPY	60
Creates a directory.	MD or MKDIR	38
Creates a disk cache.	SMARTDRV	
Creates a disk drive in memory.	RAMDRIVE	
Creates, changes, or deletes a volume label.	LABEL	
Decreases time to open frequently used files and directories.	FASTOPEN	
Deletes a directory and all subdirectories and files in it.	DELTREE	42
Deletes one or more files.	DEL or ERASE	52
Directs DOS to a labeled batch file line.	GOTO	
Displays another menu when selected from CONFIG.SYS startup menu.	SUBMENU	
Displays file and directory listing.	DIR	27
Displays HELP information.	FASTHELP	15
Displays messages, or sets command echoing on or off during execution.	ECHO	120
Displays messages (remarks) in batch files.	REM	119
Displays or changes file attributes.	ATTRIB	
Displays or sets a search path for .BAT, .EXE, and .COM files.	PATH	14
Displays or sets the active code page number.	CHCP	
Displays or sets the system date.	DATE	7
Displays or sets the system time.	TIME	7
Displays output one screen at a time.	MORE	

DOS 6.0 Command Summary

Topic or Feature	Command	Page
Displays, sets, or removes DOS environment variables.	SET	
Displays text or ASCII file contents.	TYPE	52
Displays the directory structure of a disk.	TREE	36
Displays the DOS version used to boot.	VER	
Displays the name of or changes the current directory.	CD or CHDIR	37
Displays the volume label and serial number.	VOL	
Displays used and free memory.	MEM	103
Duplicates a floppy disk.	DISKCOPY	59
Edits command lines, recalls DOS commands, and creates macros.	DOSKEY	16
Enables DOS to display an extended character set in graphics mode.	GRAFTABL	
Enables support of international character sets.	COUNTRY	
Expands compressed file(s).	EXPAND	
Formats a disk for use.	FORMAT	23
Gives detailed technical information about a computer.	MSD	131
Halts processing of a batch file temporarily.	PAUSE	119
Installs file-sharing and locking capabilities.	SHARE	
Installs keyboard and screen enhancer.	ANSI	111
Loads and runs a program above the first 64KB of memory.	LOADFIX	
Loads a program into the upper memory area.	LOADHIGH or LH	
Loads a program that can print graphics.	GRAPHICS	
Loads country-specific information.	NLSFUNC	
Loads DOS Shell.	DOSSHELL	68
Loads memory-resident program.	INSTALL	
Loads specified device driver.	DEVICE	110
Loads specified device driver into upper memory.	DEVICEHIGH	
Manages extended memory.	HIMEM	
Manages power on portable computers.	POWER	
Modifies parameters of a physical drive.	DRIVPARM	
Monitors continuously for viruses.	VSAFE	108
Moves files.	MOVE	49
Optimizes computer memory.	MEMMAKER	
Prints a text file freeing the computer to execute other DOS commands.	PRINT	
Provides CD-ROM access	MSCDEX	
Provides HELP information for DOS commands.	HELP	14
Recognizes external disk drive.	DRIVER	
Redirects I/O requests for one drive to another drive.	ASSIGN	
Removes a directory.	RD or RMDIR	41
Renames a file(s).	REN or RENAME	47
Reorganizes files to optimize a drive.	DEFRAG	63
Replaces files.	REPLACE	

Topic or Feature	Command	Page
Restores archive files that were backed up using BACKUP command with prior DOS versions.	RESTORE	
Returns to DOS Shell after a temporary exit.	EXIT	73
Runs a program testing and editing tool.	DEBUG	
Runs a specified command for each file in a set of files.	FOR	
Saves and restores the display when Task Swapper is used.	EGA	
Scans for viruses.	MSAV	108
Searches for a text string.	FIND	
Sets NumLock state in CONFIG.SYS file.	NUMLOCK	133
Sets or clears extended Ctrl+C checking.	BREAK	110
Sets the background and text colors for the CONFIG.SYS startup menu.	MENUCOLOR	133
Sets the maximum number of file control blocks that can be open concurrently.	FCBS	
Sets the maximum number of files that can be open concurrently.	FILES	110
Sets the version number reported to a program.	SETVER	
Sets up specified number of temporary I/O storage areas.	BUFFERS	110
Shifts the position of replaceable parameters in batch files.	SHIFT	
Sorts input.	SORT	
Specifies default CONFIG.SYS menu.	MENUDEFAULT	
Specifies DOS to maintain a link to upper memory area or high memory area.	DOS	
Specifies item on CONFIG.SYS startup menu.	MENUITEM	133
Specifies the maximum number of accessible disk drives.	LASTDRIVE	
Starts a new instance of the command interpreter.	COMMAND	
Starts EDIT, a screen-oriented text editor.	EDIT	96
Starts QBasic.	QBASIC	
Starts the server for INTERSVR	INTERSVR	
Supports console code-page switching.	DISPLAY	
Supports data stacks to handle hardware interrupts.	STACKS	
Supports printer code-page switching.	PRINTER	
Transfers system booting files to create a system disk.	SYS	64
Treats a disk drive as a subdirectory of another drive.	JOIN	
Treats an enhanced keyboard like a conventional keyboard.	SWITCHES	
Treats a subdirectory as a drive.	SUBST	
Treats files in an appended directory as if they were in the current directory.	APPEND	
Turns on or off EMM386 expanded memory support.	EMM386	
Undeletes files that have been deleted.	UNDELETE	91
Unformats a reformatted or restructured disk.	UNFORMAT	
Verifies while copying that files are written correctly to a disk.	VERIFY	

DOS Shell Commands

Commands without page numbers are not covered in this book.

Topic or Function	Menu	Page
Accesses HELP.	Help	76
Adds program group or program item to the command highlighted in Main area.	File ¦ New ¦ Program Group or Item	129
Associates data files with application program.	File ¦ Associate	126
Backs up disk.	Main ¦ Disk Utilities ¦ Backup Fixed Disk	
Changes attributes of highlighted file.	File ¦ Change Attributes	
Changes colors displayed in the DOS Shell.	Options ¦ Colors	
Changes confirmation choices.	Options ¦ Confirmation	87
Changes the current drive to the letter of the drive typed.	Ctrl +drive letter	71
Changes the number of lines on the monitor.	Options ¦ Display	
Changes the order in which files are listed and selectively lists files.	Options ¦ File Display Options	78
Copies highlighted file.	File ¦ Copy	88
Creates subdirectory to current directory.	File ¦ Create Directory	85
Deletes highlighted file or directory.	File ¦ Delete	87
Displays contents of highlighted file.	File ¦ View File Contents	
Displays entire disk directory structure.	Tree ¦ Expand All	77
Duplicates disk.	Main ¦ Disk Utilities ¦ Disk Copy	
Enables selection of files in different directories.	Options ¦ Select Across Directories	
Executes a command as if it were entered from the DOS prompt.	File ¦ Run	92
Executes selected program.	File ¦ Open	
Exits the DOS Shell permanently.	File ¦ Exit	73
Exits the DOS Shell temporarily.	Main ¦ Command Prompt	73
Expands the Directory Tree and File List.	View ¦ Single File List	78
Formats a disk.	Main ¦ Disk Utilities ¦ Format	85
Hides subdirectories of current directory.	Tree ¦ Collapse Branch	77
Lists all files on a drive.	View ¦ All Files	
Lists only program groups and items.	View ¦ Program List	
Loads EDIT.	Main ¦ DOS Editor	104
Moves highlighted file.	File ¦ Move	90
Opens and closes the Active Task List.	Options ¦ Enable Task Swapper	70
Prints selected text file.	File ¦ Print	
Prompts DOS to reread FAT of the current drive.	View ¦ Refresh	92

Topic or Function	Menu	Page
Removes highlighting of all previously selected files.	File ¦ Deselect All	
Removes Single or Dual File listing to display the Main area.	View ¦ Program/File Lists	78
Renames highlighted file or directory.	File ¦ Rename	86
Repaints the DOS Shell after running TSR program.	View ¦ Repaint Screen	
Restores disk.	Main ¦ Disk Utilities ¦ Restore Fixed Disk	
Searches the entire disk for the designated file.	File ¦ Search	
Selects (highlights) all files listed in File List area.	File ¦ Select All	
Shows all the subdirectories of the current directory.	Tree ¦ Expand Branch	77
Shows immediate subdirectories of the current directory.	Tree ¦ Expand One Level	77
Shows information about highlighted file and the current disk drive.	Options ¦ Show Information	
Shows two Directory Tree and File List areas.	View ¦ Dual File Lists	80
Undeletes erased file.	Main ¦ Disk Utilities ¦ Undelete	92

EDIT COMMANDS *(EDIT can be accessed from either the DOS Shell or the DOS prompt.)*

Topic or Function	Menu	Page
Accesses HELP for EDIT commands.	Help	
Clears current EDIT screen.	File ¦ New	98
Controls screen colors and Scroll Bars.	Options ¦ Display	
Copies selected text from Clipboard into document.	Edit ¦ Paste	99
Copies selected text into Clipboard.	Edit ¦ Copy	99
Deletes selected text.	Edit ¦ Clear	100
Deletes selected text from document and saves it in Clipboard.	Edit ¦ Cut	99
Exits EDIT.	File ¦ Exit	52
Opens saved file.	File ¦ Open	99
Prints current document.	File ¦ Print	100
Repeats last entered search for a specific string of characters.	Search ¦ Repeat Last Find	
Saves current document.	File ¦ Save	52
Saves current document with a new name.	File ¦ Save As	98
Searches for and replaces specified string of characters.	Search ¦ Change	
Searches for specific string of characters.	Search ¦ Find	
Searches given path for the directory containing HELP for EDIT.	Options ¦ Help Path	

Index

A

Access information on commands, 15–16
Active Task List, 69–70
/AD switch, 13, 29, 31
/AH switch, 29, 31
ALT + A keystroke, 116
ALT + B keystroke, 116
ALT + C keystroke, 116
ALT + F4 keystroke, 74, 81
ALT + F keystroke, 3, 52, 73, 81, 97
ALT + H keystroke, 76–77, 81
ALT + O keystroke, 70, 81
ALT + TAB keystroke, 105, 109
ALT + V keystroke, 70, 81
American Standard Code for Information Interchange (ASCII), 52
ANSI.SYS, 111
Area titles, 69
Arrow keys, 6, 10
ASCII. *See* American Standard Code for Information Interchange
Associate file dialog box, 126
Associate files, 126–128
/AS switch, 29, 31
Asterisk, 34–35, 43, 46, 50, 75, 81
AUTOEXEC.BAT file, 104–105

B

Backslash, 4, 12–13
BACKSPACE key, 18
"Bad command or file name" message, 5, 15
Batch files, 104, 118–120
BAT extension, 104, 119
Blinking cursor, 4
Blinking rectangle cursor, 18
Blinking underline cursor, 4, 18
Boot computer, 23
Booting, customized, 111–112
BREAK=ON, 105
BREAK, 110
Buffer, defined, 110–111
BUFFERS=number, 105
Byte, 21, 26

C

Cancel command, 10–11, 24
CAPS LOCK key, 5, 10
Caret symbol, 10
Case-sensitive, 5

CD command, 3, 37–38, 43
Central processing unit (CPU), 2
Change
    date, 7–8, 10
    directory, 3, 37–38, 43
    Directory Tree size, 78
    disks, 92
    DOS prompt, 14, 19
    drive, 27, 30, 43, 69, 80
    File List area size, 78
    filename while copying, 48, 56
    order of files, 78–79
    time, 8, 10
Characters, wild-card, 34–35
Check disk for file fragmentation, 62–63, 66
CHKDSK command, 15, 62–63, 66
CLEAR command, 100
Clear screen, 3, 5, 10
Click, 70, 81
CLS command, 3, 5, 10, 16
Cold boot, 3–5
Collapse Branch, 77
Colon, 8
COM extension, 108
Command
    advanced, 126–134
    buttons, 75
    CD (change directory), 3, 37–38, 43
    CHKDSK (check disk), 15, 62–63, 66
    CLS (clear screen), 3, 5, 10, 16
    COPY, 46–49, 56, 99
    DATE, 7–8, 10, 16
    DEFRAG (disk optimization), 63–64, 66
    DEL (delete), 52–54, 56, 96
    DELTREE, 42–43
    dimmed, 74–75
    DIR (directory), 5, 27–30
    DISKCOPY, 59–60, 65
    DOS, 12–14
    DOSKEY, 16–19, 85
    DOSSHELL, 84–93
    ECHO, 120–123
    ECHO OFF, 105–106
    EDIT, 93, 96–101
    Exit, 73–74, 81
    external, 12
    FILES, 110
    FORMAT command, 23–27, 30, 84–85
    HELP, 76–77, 81, 115–117
    internal, 12
    line, 5
    MD (make directory), 38–41, 43

147

MEM (memory), 103
MOVE, 49–50, 56
PATH, 15–16, 19, 107–109
PAUSE, 9, 11, 28, 30, 119
PRINT, 100
PROMPT, 14, 19
RD (remove directory), 41–43
Remark (REM), 119
REN (rename) , 50–51, 56
RUN, 92–93
summary, 10–11, 19, 30–31, 43, 56, 65–66, 80–81
SYS, 64–66
TIME, 8, 16
TREE, 36–37, 43
TYPE, 52, 56
XCOPY, 60–62, 65
COMMAND.COM, 23
COMMON, 133
Computer components, 1–2
Computer viruses, 106–107
CONFIG.SYS file, 104, 109–110
Config.sys menu, 132–133
Console, 2
COPY command, 46–49, 56, 99
Copy files, 46–49, 56, 65, 88–90
Copy files and directory structure, 60–62, 65
CPU. *See* Central processing unit
Create AUTOEXEC.BAT file, 104–105
Create file, 96–98
Create menu, 122–123
CTRL + ALT + DEL keystroke, 6, 10
CTRL + ASTERISK keystroke, 75, 81, 87, 89
CTRL + BREAK keystroke, 10–11
CTRL + C keystroke, 10–11, 24, 109
CTRL + drive letter, 69, 80
CTRL + ESC keystroke, 105
CTRL + INS keystroke, 96
CTRL + PRINT SCREEN keystroke, 9–11
CTRL + S keystroke, 9, 11
Current directory, 13–14, 37–39, 43
Current directory path, 68–69
Current drive, 4–5, 13–14, 43
Cursor, 4, 18, 79
Cursor movement, 6, 10
Customized booting, 111–112
Customizing system, 103–113
CUT (edit command), 99
Cycle through programs, 102

■ ■ ■ ■ ■ ■ ■ ■ ■ ■
D
Dash, 7
DATE command, 7–8, 10, 16
DBLSPACE.BIN, 23
DEFRAG command, 63–64, 66
Defragmentation, 63–64, 66
DEL command, 52–54, 56, 96
Delete character, 17

Delete file, 52–54, 56, 91
Delete Sentry, 54–55, 106
Delete Tracker, 54–55, 106
DEL key, 17, 91
DELTREE command, 42–43
Density, 21
Descending order, 79
Destination file, 46
DEVICE=C:DOSANSI.SYS, 105
Dialog boxes, 75–76
Dimmed commands, 74–75
DIR command, 5, 27–30
Directory
    command, 5, 27–30
    icons, 77
    make, 85–86
    multiple, 35–36
    names, 37
    remove, 87–88
    rename, 86–87
Directory Tree, 69, 71, 77–78, 81
DIR switches, 28–29
Disk
    integrity, 62–63, 66
    types, 21–22
DISKCOPY command, 59–60, 65
Disk drives, 2, 21–24, 69
Disk Operating System (DOS), 1
Disks, change, 92
Disk Utilities, 70, 72
Display
    commands in DOSKEY list, 17
    commands in unnumbered list, 17
    commands for which FASTHELP is available, 15, 19
    contents of file, 52, 56
    date, 7–8, 10
    directories, 29, 31, 43
    directory structure of disk, 36–37, 43
    directory structure of drive, 37, 43
    files by size, 29, 31
    files by date, 29–30
    files by extension, 28, 30
    files by filename, 13, 28, 30
    files on target drive, 29–31
    first command in DOSKEY list, 17
    hidden files, 29, 31
    last command in DOSKEY list, 17
    listing that pauses, 9, 11, 13, 28, 30
    path, 15–16, 19
    system files, 29
    time, 8, 10
    wide directory listing by extension, 28
    wide listing of files, 28, 30
Document, print, 100
DOS commands, 12–14
DOSKEY command, 16–19, 85
DOSKEY macros, 117–118
DOSKEY /MACROS, 111

DOSKEY recall keys, 17–18
DOS prompt, 4, 10
DOS. *See* Disk Operating System
DOS Shell
    access, 70, 80–81
    basics, 68–70
    cold boot, 3–4
    dialog boxes, 75–76
    Directory Tree, 69, 71, 77–78
    drop-down menus, 73–75
    exit, 73
    File List area, 69, 71–72, 78–80
    HELP, 76–77
    Main area, 72
    parts, 71–73
DOSSHELL command, 70, 80–81
Double-click, 70, 81
Double-density, 22, 27, 30
Double dot symbol, 39
Down arrow key, 17, 75
Drag, 70, 89
Drive icons, 69
Drive optimization, 63–64, 66
Drop-down menus, 73–74
Dual file listing, 81
Duplicate floppy disk, 59–60, 65

E

ECHO command, 120–123
ECHO OFF, 105–106
Edit ¦ Clear, 96
EDIT command, 51–52, 56, 93, 96–101
Edit commands
    CLEAR, 100
    COPY, 99
    CUT, 99
    HELP, 97
    PASTE, 99
Edit ¦ Copy, 96
Edit ¦ Cut, 96
Edit file, 51–52, 56
Edit ¦ Paste, 96
Edit previously entered commands, 18
Edit text, 98
Ellipses, 75
Enable system disk to work with compressed files, 23
END key, 17, 97
ENTER key, 3, 5
Erase disk, 23. *See also* Delete
Error message, 5, 15
ESC key, 17
EXE extension, 108
Exercises, 11, 20, 31–32, 44–45, 57–58, 67, 82–83
Exit command, 73–74, 81
Exit EDIT, 52, 56
Exit program to DOS Shell, 101
Expand All, 77, 81
Expand One Level, 77, 81
Extensions, multiple, 128
Extension. *See* Filename extension
External commands, 12–13
Extra-high-density, 22

F

F1 Function key, 74, 76–77, 81
F3 Function key, 3, 73, 81, 132
F5 Function key, 91, 111
F7 Function key, 17, 90
F8 Function key, 17, 88, 111
F9 Function key, 17
FASTHELP command, 15, 19
FAT. *See* File allocation table
FF. *See* Form feed button
File
    associate, 126–128
    batch, 104, 118–119
    copy, 46–49, 56, 88–90
    create, 51–52, 56, 96–98
    date, 28
    delete, 52–54, 56, 88, 91
    edit, 51–52, 56
    modify, 98–100
    move, 49–50, 56, 85, 87, 90
    rename, 50–52, 56
    reread, 89
    save, 52, 56, 97–98
    set number, 105
    size, 28
    time, 28
    undelete, 89, 91–92
File allocation table (FAT), 23
File ¦ Associate, 127
File ¦ Copy or CTRL + drag file, 87
File ¦ Copy or drag file, 85
File ¦ Create Directory, 82
File ¦ Delete, 84, 88, 131
File Display Options, 78
File ¦ Exit, 52, 56, 97
File fragmentation, 62–63, 66
File List, 69, 71–72, 78–80
File menu, 52
File ¦ Move or ALT + drag file, 87
Filename, 28, 33–34
Filename extension, 28, 33–34
File ¦ New, 95
File ¦ New ¦ Program Group, 129
File ¦ New ¦ Program Item, 130
"File not found" message, 25
File ¦ Open, 95
File ¦ Print, 97
File ¦ Properties, 131
File ¦ Rename, 83
File ¦ Run, 89
FILES command, 110

FILES=number, 105
File ¦ Save, 52, 56, 94
File ¦ Save As, 95
Floppy disk drive, 2
Floppy disk. *See* Disk
FORMAT command, 23–27, 30, 84–85
Format disk, 24–25, 30
Format double-density disk in high-density drive, 27
Form feed button (FF), 9
/F switch, 27
Function key, 70. *See also* Specific key

H

Halt command execution, 9, 11
Hard disk drive, 2
HD. *See* High-density
HELP command, 76–77, 81, 115–117
Hidden files, 29, 31
Hide commands, 102
High-density (HD), 22, 27, 30
/HISTORY command, 17
HOME key, 17, 97
Hub ring, 22

I

Input/output file requests, 23
Insert character, 17
Insert mode, 18
INS key, 17, 94, 97
Internal commands, 12
Internal disk drive, 2
Internal disk name, 25
IO.SYS, 23

K

KB. *See* Kilobyte
Key + Key keystroke, 70
Keyboard, 2, 5–6
Kilo, 22
Kilobyte (KB), 22

L

Left arrow key, 17
List directories that divide the ROOT directory, 13
List files, 5. *See also* Display
Load EDIT, 101, 105
Load internal DOS commands into memory, 23
Low-density. *See* Double-density
Lowercase, 5

M

Macros, DOSKEY, 117–118
Main area, DOS Shell, 69, 72

Main ¦ Disk Utilities, 70, 81
Main ¦ Disk Utilities ¦ Format, 82
Main ¦ Disk Utilities ¦ Undelete, 89
Main ¦ IBM or MS-DOS Editor, 101
Make directory, 38–41, 85–86
Manual feed button, 9
MB. *See* Megabyte
MD command, 38–41, 43
Mega, 22
Megabyte (MB), 22
MEM command, 103
Memory status report, 112
MENU, 122–123, 132–133
Menu Bar, 68–69
MENUCOLOR=number, 133
MENUITEM=name, 133
Metal shutter, 22
Microsoft, 1
Microsoft diagnostics command (MSD), 131–132
Minus symbol, 75, 77, 81
MODE CON: LINES=number, 107
Modify file, 98–100
Monitor, 2
"More" message, 15
Mouse, 2, 70, 72–73
Mouse pointer, 2, 69–70
MOVE command, 49–50, 56
Move cursor to left, 17
Move cursor to right, 17
Move files, 49–50, 56, 90
Move to beginning of command line, 17
Move to end of command line, 17
MSAV, 106
MSD. *See* Microsoft diagnostics command
MS-DOS, 1
MSDOS.SYS, 23
Multiple directories, 35–36
Multiple extensions, 128

N

New Program Object dialog box, 129
Nonsystem disk, 23–25
"No path" message, 26
Number of files listed, 28
Numeric keypad, 5–6
NUM LOCK key, 6, 10
NUMLOCK=OFF, 133
NUMONE, 85

O

/OD switch, 29–30
/OE switch, 28, 30
/ON switch, 13, 28, 30
Optimize disk performance, 63–64, 66
Options ¦ Confirmation, 84
Options ¦ File Display Options, 76, 81
/OS switch, 29, 31

P

PAGE DOWN key, 17, 72, 81
PAGE UP key, 17, 72, 81
Parent directory, 36, 39, 43
PASTE (edit command), 99
PATH=C:directory name;A:directory name, 103
PATH command, 15–16, 19, 107–109
PAUSE command, 9, 11, 28, 30, 119
Pause screen, 13
PC. *See* Personal computer
PC DOS, 1
Period, 7
Personal computer (PC), 1
Plus symbol, 6, 75, 77, 81
"Press any key to continue…" message, 28
Print action performed by command, 13, 19
PRINT command, 100
Print document, 100
Printer, 2
Printer echo, 9, 11
PRINT SCREEN key, 8, 11
>PRN command, 13, 19
Program/File Lists, 70, 78
Program group, 129–130
Program items, 130–131
Program Manager, 3–4
PROMPT PG, 4, 14, 19
PROMPT command, 14, 19
Prompt to enter command, 17
Protection, standard level, 55
Protection, undelete, 106
/P switch, 9, 11, 13, 28, 30

Q

Question mark, 34–35, 43, 46

R

RAM. *See* Random access memory
Random access memory (RAM), 2
RD command, 41–43
Recall last command entered with specified text, 17
Remark command (REM), 119
Remove command from DOS prompt, 17
Remove directory, 41–43, 87–88
Remove directory and erase files, 54
Remove several directories, 42–43
REM. *See* Remark command
Rename directory, 86–87
Rename file, 50–52, 56
REN command, 50–51, 56
Reorganize files on disk, 63–64, 66
Replace one character in a filename/extension, 34, 43
Replace several characters in a filename/extension, 34, 43
Reread file, 89

Restart computer, 6–7, 10
Return to Shell, 81
Review questions, 11, 19–20, 31, 44, 56, 66, 82
Right arrow key, 17
Right arrow prompt, 4. *See also* Cursor
ROOT directory, 12, 35, 38, 43
RUN command, 92–93

S

Save file, 52, 56
Scan memory and drive for viruses, 107
Screen, 2
Scroll backward, 17, 81
Scroll Bars, 69, 72
Scroll forward, 17, 81
Scrolling, 5, 81
Select disk drives, 71
Select DOS Shell area, 70–71, 80
Selection cursor, 69
Selectively list files, 79
Self-diagnostic test, 3
Serial number, 25
SHIFT + DEL keystroke, 96
SHIFT + F9 keystroke, 73, 81
SHIFT + INS keystroke, 96
SHIFT + PRINT SCREEN keystroke, 8, 11
SHIFT + TAB keystroke, 69, 80
SHIFT key, 5, 10
Show current drive, 4
Single dot symbol, 39
Single File List, 78
Size of all files listed, 28, 31
Slash, 7, 16, 40
Sort
    alphabetical order, 13, 28, 30
    date, 29–30
    filename extension, 28
    files listed, 79
    size, 31
Source file, 46
SPACEBAR, 18, 79
Special keys, 8–10
Special symbols, 5, 10, 33–34
/S switch, 25, 27, 61, 64–66
Standard level of protection, 55
Status Bar, 69
Status report on drive, 15
Strikeover mode, 18
Subdirectory, 36, 43, 77
Switch, 16
Switches, directory, 28–29
Syntax, 15
SYS command, 64–66
System date, 7–8, 25–26
System disk, 3, 23, 30, 64–66
System file listing, 29, 31
System time, 8

T

TAB key, 70, 79–81
Target drive, 29
Temporarily exit DOS Shell, 73, 81
Temporary path, 15, 19
Terminate-and-stay-resident program (TSR), 16
Text
　copy, 99
　delete, 100
　edit, 98
　move, 99
　select and deselect, 99
Three dots. *See* Ellipses
TIME command, 8, 16
Title Bar, 68–69
Toggle cursor, 18–19
Toggle key, 9–10, 79
TREE command, 36–37, 43
Tree ¦ Expand All, 77, 81
Tree ¦ Expand Branch, 77, 81
TSR. *See* Terminate-and-stay-resident program
Turn off computer, 10, 30
Turn off printer echo, 10
TXT extension, 99
TYPE command, 52, 56

U

Undelete, protection level, 106
Undelete dialog box, 91
Undelete files, 91–2
UNDELETE program, 54–56
UNDELETE /S, 106
UNDELETE /T, 106
UNDELETE /TA, 113
Unused bytes on disk, 28
Up arrow key, 17, 75
Uppercase, 5

V

View copied directory structure and files, 61–62
View ¦ Dual File Lists, 78, 81
View ¦ Program/File Lists, 76, 81
View ¦ Refresh, 89
View ¦ Single File List, 75, 81
Viruses, computer, 106–107
Volume label, 25
VSAFE, 106

W

Warm boot, 6–7, 10, 26
Wild-card characters, 34–35, 43, 46, 49–50
Write protected, 22
Write-protect notch, 22
/W switch, 28, 30

X

XCOPY command, 60–62, 65